Whole
FOOD
Slow
COOKED

Whole FOOD Slow COOKED

100 RECIPES FOR THE SLOW COOKER OR STOVETOP

OLIVIA ANDREWS

FAIR WINDS

contents

INTRODUCTION

As we become increasingly aware of the vital role that a nutritious diet based on whole foods plays in maintaining optimal health, we're demanding more and more from our everyday meals. We want a way to cook and eat that fulfills all our criteria: tasty, healthy, convenient and comforting.

In warm weather we need look no further than the salad bowl or the crisper drawer of the fridge for an easy and nourishing meal, but when the weather turns cooler, we crave thick soups, hearty stews, pasta sauces and bakes, spicy curries and dals. And then we're left searching for inspiration…not to mention the hours in our busy days to let time work its magic on such robust fare.

This is where slow cooking really comes into its own. Whether made in a dedicated slow cooker, or simply on the stovetop or in a low oven, many of these dishes virtually cook themselves. Slow cooking whole, unprocessed foods turns out to be the perfect way to make healthy, home-cooked food with maximum flavor and minimum fuss.

To provide the flexibility our busy lifestyles demand, each recipe includes cooking methods for both slow cooker and stovetop or oven, so you can choose how you want to cook. Even better, slow cooking is very forgiving. You don't need to hover over a meal as it simmers in the slow cooker (or in a low oven), and many models automatically switch to "warm" or have timers – handy if you're delayed on the way home, or the phone rings just as you come through the door!

What's more, slow cooking is economical. Because a slow cooker can spend hours cooking when you can't, you can use cheaper, more flavorful cuts of meat that need lengthy cooking to tenderize them. This means you can take advantage of special offers at the butcher or supermarket. To make shopping and cooking even easier, we've given alternative cuts of meat that can be substituted in each recipe, and also included specific cuts in the index, so you can look up dishes to cook with whatever you've got.

You will notice that many of the recipes in the book are scattered with freshly chopped herbs before serving, and that sometimes we suggest an accompaniment such as a crunchy gremolata. Stews and braises made in the slow cooker do indeed become meltingly tender, often with a velvety sauce, so you will find that the addition of a little fresh herby crispness, crunch or spice for serving will add contrast and finish the dish perfectly.

For many of us, the time it takes to cook dried beans and legumes is prohibitive, especially during the week. But with a slow cooker, you can cook soaked dried beans from scratch, rather than resorting to the more expensive quick-fix of canned beans, which can also be laden with salt and sugar. Talking of sugar, there's no need to miss out on a sweet treat either, as these recipes use only unrefined sugars or healthier alternatives such as rice syrup, agave syrup or honey to create comforting puddings and cakes (several of which do double-duty as both dessert and afternoon pick-me-up).

If you're investing in your first slow cooker, there are a few things to keep in mind. The capacity of slow cookers ranges from modest versions, perfect for small households, to bigger models (up to 7½ quarts/7 L) that will feed a crowd, often with a meal or two left over for the freezer as well. The majority of the recipes in this book were developed using slow cookers with a capacity between 5 to 6½ quarts (5 to 6.5 L), but for most recipes the size won't make any difference. When making gratins or cakes, however, the dimensions of your slow cooker may affect the cooking time, so we've given guidance on the size of slow cooker needed in the introductions to these recipes. And, of course, if you want to cook large joints such as a lamb shoulder or leg, or a whole chicken or fish, you'll need a slow cooker big enough to hold them. Of course, if your slow cooker isn't big enough you can still cook these dishes in the oven or on the stovetop, with equally delicious results.

Dishes made in the slow cooker need less liquid added than those cooked on the stovetop or in the oven, as the liquid cannot evaporate. (As a general rule, you'll need about half the amount of liquid in the slow cooker.) For the same reason, it's important to let the cooking liquid simmer, uncovered, for a few minutes after adding wine, beer or spirits, in order to cook off the alcohol and soften its harsh taste. Some recipes will also ask you to place a circle of parchment paper, cut to size, directly on the surface of the liquid in a slow cooker or casserole, to keep ingredients submerged so they cook evenly without drying out. Since slow cookers take a while to heat up, resist the urge to lift the lid during cooking; if you do need to stir or check the food, replace the lid as soon as possible so the slow cooker doesn't lose too much heat.

As with any kitchen equipment, there are some safety points to remember when using your slow cooker:

- Never cook any meat from frozen, or partially frozen, in a slow cooker, as this can allow food-poisoning bacteria to multiply. *Always* thaw meat fully before cooking.
- If your slow cooker's ceramic insert has been refrigerated or frozen, let it come to room temperature before cooking, or the sudden change in temperature could cause it to crack.
- Never cook dried kidney-shaped beans from their raw state in a slow cooker, as the temperature won't be high enough to destroy the natural toxin found in these beans. Canned beans are safe for immediate use, but dried red kidney beans (and other similar-shaped beans) should be soaked overnight, then boiled vigorously in fresh water for 10 minutes before being added to the slow cooker. We've included these instructions in all the relevant recipes, but don't forget this step if you're adapting other recipes for your slow cooker.
- Finally, as all slow cookers are slightly different, make sure you read the manufacturer's instructions for the safe use of your particular model.

And that's it! Follow these simple guidelines and you'll enjoy an amazing variety of wholesome and delicious meals from your slow cooker.

Sharing tricks of the trade and convenient shortcuts without compromising on flavor or authenticity, these are recipes you'll come back to again and again. Soon you'll wonder why you ever cooked any other way.

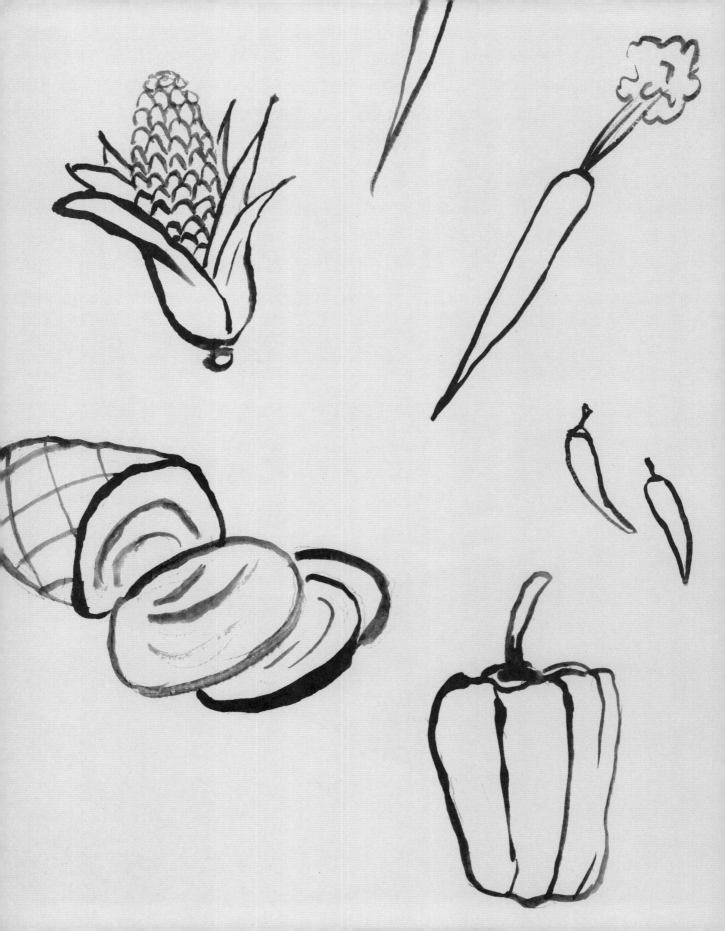

family
favorites

CARAMEL PORK BELLY

If you want to garnish this with crispy Thai basil, briefly fry a handful of the leaves in a little oil until translucent; if you can't find Thai basil, just scatter some regular basil or cilantro leaves over the top instead. Look for rice malt syrup in health food shops.

SERVES: 6

Preparation time: 10 minutes
Cooking time: 4¾ hours (slow cooker)
1 hour 50 minutes (stovetop)

1 tablespoon (15 ml) grapeseed or rice bran oil
3 lb 5 oz (1.5 kg) skinless pork belly,
    cut into 2 inch (5 cm) pieces
3 tablespoons (45 ml) kecap manis Indonesian
    sweet soysauce
¾ cup (6 fl oz/185 ml) rice malt syrup
1 teaspoon ground white or black pepper
1 teaspoon ground ginger
1 teaspoon ground cinnamon
4 cloves garlic, crushed
3 tablespoons (45 ml) fish sauce
4 star anise
1 cup (9 fl oz/250 ml) chicken stock
1 teaspoon cornstarch – only needed for slow
    cooker
1 small bunch snake beans or a handful of green
    beans, cut into 2 inch (5 cm) lengths
steamed rice, Thai basil and sliced chili,
    to serve

IN THE SLOW COOKER

Heat the oil in a large frying pan or wok over high heat. Cook the pork for 5 minutes until browned.

Meanwhile, combine the kecap manis, syrup, pepper, ginger, cinnamon, garlic, fish sauce and star anise in a bowl. Pour the mixture into the pan and cook for 3 minutes to glaze the pork. Transfer to the slow cooker.

Combine the chicken stock and cornflour in a bowl until smooth, then add to the slow cooker and stir well. Cook on high for 4 hours.

Skim any fat from the surface, then add the beans and cook for a further 30 minutes.

Serve with steamed rice, Thai basil and chili.

ON THE STOVETOP

Heat the oil in a large frying pan or wok over high heat. Cook the pork for 5 minutes until browned.

Meanwhile, combine the kecap manis, syrup, pepper, ginger, cinnamon, garlic, fish sauce, star anise and stock in a bowl. Pour the mixture into the pan, bring to a boil, then reduce the heat to low. Cover with a lid and cook for 90 minutes until the pork is tender.

Skim any fat from the surface, then stir in the beans and cook for 10 minutes until tender.

Serve with steamed rice, Thai basil and chili.

SPLIT GREEN PEA AND HAM SOUP

This comforting family favorite is given extra zip with frozen peas and fresh mint.

SERVES: 4–6

Preparation time: 10 minutes
Cooking time: 7¼ hours (slow cooker)
3¼ hours (stovetop)

1 tablespoon (15 ml) olive oil
1 onion, finely chopped
1 carrot, cut into ¾ inch (2 cm) cubes
2 cloves garlic, finely chopped
2 cups (15½ oz/440 g) split green peas, rinsed
1 smoked ham hock
1 fresh or dried bay leaf
6 sprigs thyme, tied in a bundle with string
4 cups (35 fl oz/1 L) chicken stock
2 cups (10 oz/280 g) frozen peas, thawed
mint leaves and crusty bread, to serve

IN THE SLOW COOKER

Heat the oil in a large saucepan over medium heat. Cook the onion, carrot and garlic for 5 minutes until softened. Transfer to the slow cooker with the split green peas, ham hock, bay leaf, thyme, stock and 3 cups (26 fl oz/ 750 ml) of water. Cook on low for 6 hours.

Remove the ham hock and set aside, then turn the slow cooker to high. When the ham hock is cool enough to handle, roughly shred the meat, discarding the skin and bones. Return the meat to the slow cooker and stir well. Cook for 30 minutes until the split peas and ham are tender.

Meanwhile, roughly mash half of the thawed peas with the back of a fork. Once the split peas and ham are tender, stir in the peas and cook for a further 10 minutes until warmed through. Remove and discard the thyme. Season to taste with salt and pepper.

Serve with mint leaves and crusty bread.

ON THE STOVETOP

Heat the oil in a large saucepan over medium heat. Cook the onion, carrot and garlic for 5 minutes until softened. Add the split green peas, ham hock, bay leaf, thyme, stock and 4 cups (35 fl oz/1 L) of water and bring to a boil. Reduce the heat to a simmer, cover with a lid and cook for 2 hours, turning the hock halfway through, until the meat is tender.

Remove the ham hock and set aside until cool enough to handle. Roughly shred the meat, discarding the skin and bones, then return to the pan and stir well. Cook for 30 minutes until the split peas and ham are tender.

Meanwhile, roughly mash half of the thawed peas with the back of a fork. Once the split peas and ham are tender, stir in the peas and cook for a further 5 minutes until warmed through. Remove and discard the thyme. Season to taste with salt and pepper.

Serve with mint leaves and crusty bread.

VEAL OSSO BUCO WITH KALE GREMOLATA

This delicious Italian casserole has been brought up to date with a kale gremolata. You will need at least a 5-quart (175 fl oz/5 L) slow cooker for this recipe.

SERVES: 4

Preparation time: 15 minutes
Cooking time: 7¼ hours (slow cooker)
2¼ hours (oven)

3 tablespoons (45 ml) olive oil
⅓ cup (1¾ oz/50 g) all-purpose flour
2 lb 12 oz (1.2 kg) veal osso buco
2 onions, halved, thinly sliced
1 cinnamon stick
½ teaspoon ground allspice
1 cup (9 fl oz/250 ml) dry white wine
2 tomatoes, coarsely chopped
3 tablespoons (12 g) coarsely chopped oregano
2 cups (17 fl oz/500 ml) chicken stock
2 fresh or dried bay leaves
finely grated zest of 1 lemon
¾ cup (4¾ oz/130 g) Sicilian green olives, pitted
creamy polenta or potato mash, to serve

Kale gremolata
1 cup (2¾ oz/75 g) finely chopped kale
1 clove garlic, finely chopped
juice and finely grated zest of ½ lemon
1 tablespoon (15 ml) extra virgin olive oil

IN THE SLOW COOKER

Heat half of the oil in a large, heavy-based saucepan over medium–high heat. Place the flour in a bowl and season with salt and pepper. Dust the osso buco in the flour and cook for 5 minutes until browned. Transfer to the slow cooker. Reduce the heat to medium and add the remaining oil to the pan. Add the onions, cinnamon and allspice and cook for 4 minutes until the onions have softened. Add the wine and let it boil for 3 minutes to evaporate the alcohol, then transfer the mixture to the slow cooker, along with the tomatoes, oregano, stock, bay leaves and lemon zest. Season well with salt and pepper. Cook on low for 6 hours, then gently stir in the olives. Cook for a further hour until the meat is falling off the bone.

Meanwhile, for the gremolata, combine the ingredients in a bowl. Season with salt and pepper, then set aside for at least 30 minutes to allow the lemon juice to soften the kale.

Serve with polenta or mash and the gremolata.

IN THE OVEN

Preheat the oven to 300°F/gas mark 2 (150°C). Heat half of the oil in a large, ovenproof saucepan over medium–high heat. Place the flour in a bowl and season with salt and pepper. Dust the osso buco in the flour and cook for 5 minutes until browned. Remove and set aside. Reduce the heat to medium and add the remaining oil to the pan. Add the onions, cinnamon and allspice and cook for 4 minutes until the onions have softened.

Return the osso buco to the pan, along with the tomatoes, oregano, wine, bay leaves and lemon zest. Season well with salt and pepper. Bring to a boil and let it bubble for 1 minute, then add the stock and return to the boil. Cover with a lid and place in the oven for 90 minutes. Add the olives and cook for a further 30 minutes until the meat is tender.

Meanwhile, for the gremolata, combine the ingredients in a bowl. Season with salt and pepper, then set aside for at least 30 minutes to allow the lemon juice to soften the kale.

Serve with polenta or mash and the gremolata.

TARRAGON CHICKEN WITH 40 GARLIC CLOVES

This brings together two classic French dishes to create something that's a step above the typical roast chuck dinner. You'll need a large slow cooker for this – or just pop it in the oven.

SERVES: 4

Preparation time: 15 minutes
Cooking time: 3¼ hours (slow cooker)
2½ hours (oven)

1–2 tablespoons (15–30 ml) extra virgin olive oil
2 French shallots, finely chopped
1 teaspoon yellow mustard seeds
3 tablespoons (50 g) butter, softened
3 tablespoons (12 g) coarsely chopped tarragon
3 lb 8 oz (1.6 kg) chicken, excess fat removed
1 onion, thickly sliced
1 large carrot, peeled, quartered lengthwise
3 waxy potatoes, peeled, cut into large pieces
40 cloves garlic, unpeeled
2 cups (17 fl oz/500 ml) chicken stock
crusty bread and green salad, to serve

IN THE SLOW COOKER

Heat 1 tablespoon (15 ml) of the oil in a frying pan over medium heat. Cook the shallots and mustard seeds for 3 to 5 minutes until the shallots have softened and are lightly golden. Set aside to cool.

Meanwhile, combine the butter and tarragon in a bowl. Add the shallot mixture to the bowl, season with salt and pepper and mix well.

Slide your fingers between the skin and the breasts of the chicken to gently loosen and create two pockets. Spread the tarragon butter evenly under the chicken skin.

Heat the remaining oil in a large frying pan over medium–high heat. Cook the chicken, turning, for 5 minutes until browned.

Meanwhile, layer the onion, carrot and potatoes in the slow cooker. Add 8 garlic cloves to the cavity of the chicken, then place the bird in the slow cooker with the remaining garlic and stock. Season with salt and pepper, then cook on high for 3 hours.

Serve with crusty bread and green salad.

IN THE OVEN

Heat 1 tablespoon oil (15 ml) in a small frying pan over medium heat. Cook the shallots and mustard seeds for 3 to 5 minutes until the shallots have softened and are lightly golden. Set aside to cool.

Preheat the oven to 400°F/gas mark 6 (200°C).

Meanwhile, combine the butter and tarragon in a bowl. Add the shallot mixture to the bowl, season with salt and pepper and mix well.

Slide your fingers between the skin and the breasts of the chicken to gently loosen and create two pockets. Spread the tarragon butter evenly under the chicken skin.

Lay the onion, carrot and potatoes over the base of a large roasting tin. Add 8 garlic cloves to the cavity of the chicken, then place the bird in the pan with the remaining garlic and stock. Season with salt and pepper. Cook in the oven for 15 minutes, then reduce the temperature to 300°F/gas mark 2 (150°C) and cook for a further 2 hours until the juices run clear when a skewer is inserted into the thickest part of the thigh. Loosely cover with foil if the skin is browning too much.

Serve with crusty bread and green salad.

BEEF BURGUNDY

This traditional French beef cassserole is rich and full of flavor. If you don't have speck or pancetta, just use bacon.

SERVES: 4–6

Preparation time: 20 minutes
Cooking time: 6½ hours (slow cooker)
2½ hours (stovetop)

¼ cup (60 ml) olive oil
5½ ounces (150 g) rindless speck or pancetta, cut into lardons
⅓ cup (1¾ oz/50 g) all-purpose flour
2 lb 4 oz (1 kg) beef chuck steak, cut into 2 inch (5 cm) cubes
3 tablespoons (40 g) butter
2 carrots, peeled, halved lengthwise, thickly sliced
1 leek, pale green and white parts only, halved lengthwise then thinly sliced
12 small shallots, peeled, halved
2 cloves garlic, finely chopped
2 fresh or dried bay leaves
8 sprigs thyme, leaves picked
7 ounces (200 g) chestnut or button mushrooms, quartered
1 bottle of red wine, such as burgundy
green beans and potato mash, to serve

IN THE SLOW COOKER

Heat 1 tablespoon (15 ml) of the oil in a large frying pan over medium–high heat. Cook the speck for 2 minutes until lightly golden, then transfer to the slow cooker.

Meanwhile, put the flour in a bowl and season with salt and pepper. Lightly dust the beef in the flour to coat, shaking off any excess.

Add another 1 tablespoon (15 ml) of the oil to the pan and cook the beef for 5 minutes until browned. Transfer to the slow cooker.

Add 1 tablespoon (15 ml) of the oil and half of the butter to the pan, then cook the carrots, leek and shallots for 3 minutes until lightly golden. Transfer to the slow cooker.

Heat the remaining oil and butter in the pan. Add the garlic, bay leaves, thyme and mushrooms and cook for 2 minutes. Add the wine to the pan and boil for 8 minutes to evaporate the alcohol. Transfer to the slow cooker and cook on low for 6 hours until the beef is tender. Check the seasoning.

Serve with green beans and potato mash.

ON THE STOVETOP

Put the flour in a bowl and season with salt and pepper. Lightly dust the beef in the flour to coat, shaking off any excess.

Meanwhile, heat half of the butter and half of the oil in a large, heavy-based saucepan over medium–high heat. Cook the beef for 5 minutes until browned, then remove and set aside. Add the speck and cook for 2 minutes until lightly golden. Add the remaining butter and oil and reduce the heat to medium, then cook the carrots, leek and shallots for 5 minutes until lightly golden. Add the garlic, bay leaves and thyme and cook for a further minute. Add the wine to the pan and boil for 8 minutes to evaporate the alcohol.

Return the beef to the pan, along with 1 cup (9 fl ounces/250 ml) of water and bring to a boil. Season with salt and pepper, then reduce the heat to a simmer, cover with a lid and cook for 1½ hours until the beef is almost tender. Add the mushrooms and cook for a further 30 minutes. Check the seasoning.

Serve with green beans and potato mash.

CHICKEN AND VEGETABLE PIE

If you want to get a head start with this, freeze the filling before adding the peas, parsley and crème fraîche. It will keep in an airtight container for up to a month.

SERVES: 6

Preparation time: 20 minutes
Cooking time: 5½ hours (slow cooker)
1½ hours (stovetop)

½ cup (2¼ oz/60 g) cornstarch
2 lb 4 oz (1 kg) chicken thigh fillets,
    cut into 1¼ inch (3 cm) pieces
3 tablespoons (45 ml) olive oil
1½ tablespoons (20 g) butter
2 slices bacon, coarsely chopped
2 leeks, halved lengthwise, thinly sliced
2 stalks celery, cut into ½ inch (1 cm) slices
2 cloves garlic, finely chopped
1 cup (9 fl oz/250 ml) chicken stock
2 corn cobs, kernels cut from cobs
6 puff pastry sheets
1 egg, lightly beaten
1 cup (5 oz/140 g) frozen peas
handful coarsely chopped parsley
3 tablespoons (45 g) crème fraîche or sour cream

IN THE SLOW COOKER

Put the cornstarch in a bowl and season with salt and pepper, then coat the chicken pieces.

Heat 2 tablespoons (30 ml) of the oil in large frying pan over medium–high heat. In batches, cook the chicken for 5 minutes, turning, until golden. Transfer to the slow cooker.

Add the remaining oil and butter to the pan. Cook the bacon, leeks, celery and garlic for 4 minutes until the leeks have softened. Transfer to the slow cooker with the stock and corn. Season with salt and pepper, then cook on low for 5 hours until tender.

Meanwhile, preheat the oven to 350°F/gas mark 4 (180°C). Pleat the edges of each pastry sheet into a rough circle. Place on 3 large, lined baking sheets and brush with

the egg. Bake in the oven for 25 to 30 minutes until golden and cooked through.

Add the parsley, peas and crème fraîche to the slow cooker. Stir in, then leave to cook for 10 minutes until warmed through.

Serve topped with the pastry lids.

ON THE STOVETOP

Put the cornstarch in a bowl and season with salt and pepper, then coat the chicken pieces.

Heat 2 tablespoons (30 ml) of the oil in large, heavy-based saucepan over medium–high heat. In batches, cook the chicken for 5 minutes, turning, until golden. Remove and set aside.

Add the remaining oil and butter to the pan. Cook the bacon, leeks, celery and garlic for 4 minutes until the leeks have softened. Add the stock, corn, 1 cup (9 fl oz/250 ml) of water and return the chicken to the pan. Season with salt and pepper. Bring to a boil, then cover with a lid and reduce the heat to low. Simmer for 1 hour, stirring occasionally, then remove the lid and cook for 15 minutes.

Meanwhile, preheat the oven to 350°F/gas mark 4 (180°C). Pleat the edges of each pastry sheet into a rough circle. Place on 3 large, lined baking sheets and brush with the egg. Bake in the oven for 25 to 30 minutes until golden and cooked through.

Stir the parsley, peas and crème fraîche into the pan and cook for 5 minutes until warmed through.

Serve topped with the pastry lids.

BEST EVER MEATLOAF

You can hide vegetables from the kids in this meatloaf! They'll love its savory taste and sticky tomato glaze so much that they'll never suspect.

SERVES: 4–6

Preparation time: 10 minutes
Cooking time: 4 hours (slow cooker)
1¼ hours (oven)

1 lb 5 oz (600 g) ground beef
14 oz (400 g) ground pork
¾ cup (2¾ oz/75 g) rolled oats
1 egg, lightly beaten
½ cup (1¾ oz/50 g) finely grated parmesan
1 carrot, coarsely grated
1 zucchini, coarsely grated
2 cloves garlic, finely chopped
handful finely chopped basil

Tomato glaze
1 jar (1 lb 9 oz/700 g) tomato passata
1 tablespoon (11 g) dijon mustard
3 tablespoons (45 ml) maple syrup
2 tablespoons (30 ml) Worcestershire sauce
1 tablespoon (15 ml) apple cider vinegar
potato mash and wilted spinach, to serve

IN THE SLOW COOKER

Grease and line the slow cooker with parchment paper. Put all the ingredients in a bowl, season with salt and pepper and mix well. Evenly press the meatloaf mixture into the slow cooker. Cook on low for 4 hours or until cooked through and the meatloaf is coming away from the sides.

Meanwhile, for the tomato glaze, put all the ingredients in a saucepan over medium heat. Bring to the boil, then reduce the heat to a simmer and cook for 15 minutes until thickened. Season to taste.

Turn out the meatloaf and pour over the glaze, then serve with potato mash and wilted spinach.

IN THE OVEN

Preheat the oven to 325°F/gas mark 3 (170°C). Put all the ingredients in a bowl, season with salt and pepper, and mix well. Transfer the mixture to a large roasting tin, then use your hands to mold into a meatloaf shape. Bake in the oven for 1¼ hours until cooked through.

Meanwhile, for the tomato glaze, put all the ingredients in a saucepan over medium heat. Bring to a boil, then reduce the heat to a simmer and cook for 15 minutes until thickened. Season to taste.

Turn out the meatloaf and pour over the glaze, then serve with potato mash and wilted spinach.

ULTIMATE BOLOGNESE

ULTIMATE BOLOGNESE

Pork sausages are a great way to pack your bolognese with flavor, but you could easily use ground pork instead. For added depth, feel free to add a glass of red wine or even chopped anchovy fillets at the same time as the tomato paste.

SERVES: 6

Preparation time: 10 minutes
Cooking time: 8¼ hours (slow cooker)
3¼ hours (stovetop)

1 tablespoon (15 ml) extra virgin olive oil
1 lb 10 oz (750 g) ground beef
9 oz (250 g) Italian pork sausages,
   casings removed
4 slices bacon, coarsely chopped
¾ oz (20 g) butter
2 red onions, finely chopped
1 large carrot, finely chopped
2 stalks celery, finely chopped
2 cloves garlic, finely chopped
3 tablespoons (45 g) tomato paste
2 cans (14 oz/400 g) chopped tomatoes
1½ cups (13 fl oz/375 ml) beef stock
1 teaspoon raw sugar
2 fresh or dried bay leaves
6 thyme sprigs, leaves picked
pasta, chopped parsley and grated parmesan,
   to serve

IN THE SLOW COOKER

Heat the oil in a large, heavy-based saucepan over medium–high heat. Cook the beef, sausage and bacon for 5 minutes or until browned, breaking up the meat with a wooden spoon. Drain any liquid from the pan and transfer the meat to the slow cooker.

Reduce the heat to medium and melt the butter in the pan. Add the onions, carrot, celery and garlic and cook for 3 minutes until slightly softened. Add the tomato paste and cook for 3 minutes, stirring. Transfer the mixture to the slow cooker, along with the remaining ingredients.

Cook on low for 8 hours, then skim off any fat that has risen to the surface. Season to taste with salt and pepper.

Serve with pasta, parsley and parmesan.

ON THE STOVETOP

Heat the oil in a large, heavy-based saucepan over medium–high heat. Cook the beef, sausage and bacon for 5 minutes or until browned, breaking up the meat with a wooden spoon. Transfer the meat to a bowl.

Reduce the heat to medium and melt the butter in the pan. Add the onions, carrot, celery and garlic and cook for 3 minutes until slightly softened. Add the tomato paste and cook for 3 minutes, stirring.

Return the meat to the pan, along with the remaining ingredients. Bring to a boil for 5 minutes, then reduce the heat to low, cover with a lid and simmer, stirring occasionally, for 2½ hours. Remove the lid and cook for a further 30 minutes until the meat is very tender and the sauce has thickened. Season to taste with salt and pepper.

Serve with pasta, parsley and parmesan.

CHILI CON CARNE

This much-loved and versatile chili con carne works well in tacos, burritos or spooned over nachos. It also freezes well.

SERVES: 4

Preparation time: 5 minutes + overnight soaking
Cooking time: 7½ hours (slow cooker)
2¾ hours (stovetop)

¾ cup (5½ oz/150 g) dried pinto or borlotti beans, soaked overnight, drained and rinsed
1 tablespoon olive oil
1 onion, finely chopped
2 cloves garlic, finely chopped
1 lb 2 oz (500 g) ground beef
1 red pepper, cut into ½ inch (1 cm) dice
2 teaspoons chili powder
2 teaspoons ground cumin
2 teaspoons smoked paprika
1 teaspoon dried oregano
2 tablespoons (30 g) tomato paste
2 cans (14 oz/400 g) chopped tomatoes
1 teaspoon raw sugar – optional
2 fresh or dried bay leaves
1 cup (9 fl oz/250 ml) beef stock
corn, cilantro, green chili, lime and corn chips or steamed rice, to serve

IN THE SLOW COOKER

Put the beans into a large saucepan, cover with water and bring to a boil. Cook for 15 minutes, then drain the beans and tip into the slow cooker.

Meanwhile, heat the oil in a large, deep frying pan over medium heat. Cook the onion and garlic for 3 minutes or until slightly softened. Add the beef, pepper, spices and oregano and season with salt. Cook for 5 minutes or until the beef has browned. Add the tomato paste and cook for a minute, then transfer to the slow cooker, along with the remaining ingredients. Cook on low for 7 hours until the beans are tender. Check the seasoning.

Serve with corn, cilantro, green chili, lime and corn chips or steamed rice.

ON THE STOVETOP

Put the beans into a large saucepan, cover with water and bring to a boil. Cook for 20 minutes, then drain and set aside.

Meanwhile, heat the oil in a large, heavy-based saucepan over medium heat. Cook the onion and garlic for 3 minutes or until slightly softened. Add the beef, pepper, spices and oregano and season with salt. Cook for 5 minutes or until the beef has browned. Add the tomato paste and cook for a minute, then add the canned tomatoes, sugar, bay leaves, stock and 1 cup (9 fl oz/ 250 ml) of water and bring to a boil. Reduce the heat to low, cover with a lid and cook for 1½ hours. Add the beans and cook for a further 30 minutes until the beans are tender, stirring occasionally and adding more water if needed. Check the seasoning.

Serve with corn, cilantro, green chili, lime and corn chips or steamed rice.

PULLED PORK

These succulent pulled pork sandwiches are always a big hit. Any leftovers can be frozen in an airtight container for up to a month and used in wraps and tacos, or on top of a baked potato.

SERVES: 6

Preparation time: 5 minutes
Cooking time: 8¼ hours (slow cooker)
4¼ hours (oven)

1 tablespoon (7 g) smoked paprika
1 teaspoon ground white or black pepper
1 teaspoon chili flakes
1 teaspoon onion powder
1 teaspoon garlic powder
1 teaspoon mustard powder
1 tablespoon maple syrup
3 lb 5 oz (1.5 kg) pork shoulder,
    cut into large pieces
1 cup (9 fl oz/250 ml) apple juice
3 tablespoons (45 ml) apple cider vinegar
coleslaw and soft buns, to serve

IN THE SLOW COOKER

Combine the paprika, pepper, chili, onion, garlic and mustard powders, maple syrup and 2 teaspoons salt in a bowl to make a spice paste. Put the pork into the slow cooker. Using your hands, rub the pork with the spice paste. Pour in the apple juice and vinegar, then cook on low for 8 hours until tender. Remove the pork from the slow cooker, "pull" the meat by shredding it with two forks, then return to the slow cooker for 15 minutes until warmed through.

Serve with coleslaw and soft buns.

IN THE OVEN

Preheat the oven to 300°F/gas mark 2 (150°C). Combine the paprika, pepper, chili, onion, garlic and mustard powders, maple syrup and 2 teaspoons salt in a bowl. Put the pork into a large ovenproof saucepan. Using your hands, rub the pork with the spice paste. Pour in the apple juice and vinegar, then cover with a lid and roast in the oven for 4 hours until tender. Remove the pork from the oven, "pull" the meat by shredding it with two forks, then return to the oven for 10 to 15 minutes until warmed through.

Serve with coleslaw and soft buns.

POTATO, WHITE CHEESE AND PROSCIUTTO GRATIN

With three cheeses and prosciutto, this indulgent potato gratin is a real winter warmer. If you're making it in a slow cooker, keep in mind that the potatoes may take slightly more or less time to become tender, depending on the size of your slow cooker, so check them every now and again.

SERVES: 4–6

Preparation time: 20 minutes
Cooking time: 6¼ hours (slow cooker)
1¾ hours (oven)

3 tablespoons (40 g) butter
2 tablespoons all-purpose flour
2 cups (17 fl oz/500 ml) milk
9 oz (250 g) mascarpone
9 oz (250 g) cottage cheese
9 oz (200 g) creamy feta, crumbled
3½ oz (100 g) prosciutto slices, finely chopped
2 lb 12 oz (1.2 kg) waxy potatoes, very thinly sliced
toasted breadcrumbs, chopped parsley and green salad, to serve

IN THE SLOW COOKER

Melt the butter in a saucepan over medium heat. Add the flour and cook for 1 minute until foaming, then gradually whisk in the milk and keep whisking until the sauce thickens. Stir in the mascarpone, cottage cheese, feta and prosciutto, then season with salt and pepper. Cook for a further 5 minutes until thickened.

Lightly grease the slow cooker. Arrange two layers of potatoes in the slow cooker and spread over ½ cup (4 fl oz/125 ml) of the cheese mixture to cover. Repeat these layers until all the potatoes and cheese are used up, ending with the cheese mixture. Cook on high for 6 hours until the potatoes are tender.

Serve with toasted breadcrumbs, chopped parsley and green salad.

IN THE OVEN

Preheat the oven to 350°F/gas mark 4 (180°C).

Melt the butter in a saucepan over medium heat. Add the flour and cook for 1 minute until foaming, then gradually whisk in the milk and keep whisking until the sauce thickens. Stir in the mascarpone, cottage cheese, feta and prosciutto, then season with salt and pepper. Cook for a further 5 minutes until thickened.

Lightly grease a 13 x 9-inch (33 x 23 cm) baking dish. Arrange two layers of potatoes in the base of the dish and spread over ½ cup (4 fl oz/125 ml) of the cheese mixture to cover. Repeat these layers until all the potatoes and cheese are used up, ending with the cheese mixture.

Cover the dish tightly with foil and bake the gratin in the oven for 45 minutes, then remove the foil and cook for another 45 minutes until the potato is tender.

Serve with toasted breadcrumbs, chopped parsley and green salad.

IRISH LAMB, BARLEY AND POTATO STEW

For a less authentic, but equally tasty, variation use farro instead of the barley. And, if you want a gluten-free Irish stew, just leave out the grains altogether.

SERVES: 4

Preparation time: 5 minutes
Cooking time: 7¼ hours (slow cooker)
1½ hours (stovetop)

2 tablespoons (30 ml) olive oil
1 lb 10 oz (750 g) lamb neck, trimmed,
  cut into 1½ inch (4 cm) pieces
½ cup (3½ oz/100 g) pearl barley, rinsed
1 onion, finely chopped
2 carrots, thickly sliced
1 large stalk celery, coarsely chopped
1 lb 2 oz (500 g) potatoes, cut into
  1¼ inch (3 cm) pieces
2 cups (17 fl oz/500 ml) chicken stock
2 cups (5½ oz/150 g) coarsely chopped
  savoy cabbage
chopped parsley, to serve

IN THE SLOW COOKER

Heat 1 tablespoon (15 ml) of the oil in a large frying pan over medium–high heat. Season the lamb with salt and pepper, then cook for 5 minutes until browned. Transfer to the slow cooker, along with the barley.

Reduce the heat to medium, add the remaining oil to the pan and cook the onion for 3 minutes until slightly softened. Transfer to the slow cooker, together with the carrots, celery, potatoes, stock and 1 cup (9 fl oz/ 250 ml) of water. Cook on low for 6 hours, then add the cabbage and cook for a further hour until everything is tender.

Serve with chopped parsley.

ON THE STOVETOP

Heat 1 tablespoon (15 ml) of the oil in a large, heavy-based saucepan over medium–high heat. Season the lamb with salt and pepper, then cook for 5 minutes until browned. Remove and set aside. Reduce the heat to medium, add the remaining oil to the pan and cook the onion for 3 minutes until slightly softened.

Stir in the barley, stock and 2 cups (17 fl oz/ 500 ml) of water and bring to a boil. Cover with a lid, reduce the heat to low and cook for 45 minutes. Add the carrots and celery and cook for another 15 minutes. Add the cabbage and potatoes, ensuring all the ingredients are submerged – add a little more water if necessary. Bring to a boil, then cover with the lid and cook for a further 15 to 20 minutes until everything is tender.

Serve with chopped parsley.

soups

SQUASH AND RED LENTIL SOUP

Any orange-fleshed squash, such as butternut, works well in this soothing and nourishing soup. If you can't find lemon thyme, just use regular thyme.

SERVES: 4–6

Preparation time: 15 minutes
Cooking time: 4 hours (slow cooker)
40 minutes (stovetop)

1 tablespoon (15 ml) olive oil
1½ tablespoon (20 g) butter
1 brown onion, coarsely chopped
2 cloves garlic, finely chopped
½ teaspoon chili powder
¼ teaspoon ground nutmeg
1 fresh or dried bay leaf
4 sprigs lemon thyme, leaves picked
2 lb 12 oz (1.2 kg) squash, seeds removed, peeled,
    cut into 1¼ inch (3 cm) cubes
1 cup (7 oz/200 g) red lentils, rinsed
4 cups (35 fl oz/1 L) chicken or vegetable stock
Greek-style yogurt and toasted pepitas
    (pumpkin seeds), to serve

IN THE SLOW COOKER

Heat the oil and butter in a frying pan over medium heat. Cook the onion for 3 minutes until slightly softened, then add the garlic, chili, nutmeg, bay leaf and thyme and cook for a further 2 minutes until fragrant. Transfer to the slow cooker, along with the pumpkin, lentils, stock and 1 cup (9 fl oz/250 ml) of water. Season with salt and pepper, then cook on high for 4 hours until the squash and lentils are tender.

Using a stick blender, purée the soup until smooth. Check the seasoning, then serve with yogurt and toasted pepitas.

ON THE STOVETOP

Heat the oil and butter in a large, heavy-based saucepan over medium heat. Cook the onion for 3 minutes until slightly softened, then add the garlic, chili, nutmeg, bay leaf and thyme and cook for a further 2 minutes until fragrant. Add the squash, lentils, stock and 2 cups (17 fl oz/500 ml) of water. Season with salt and pepper. Bring to a boil, then reduce the heat to a simmer and cover with a lid. Cook for 30 minutes until the squash and lentils are tender.

Using a stick blender, purée the soup until smooth, adding more water if necessary. Check the seasoning, then serve with yogurt and toasted pepitas.

GREEK CHICKEN SOUP WITH RICE AND LEMON

Behind every delicious chicken soup there's always a good chicken stock! With the zestiness of lemon and a handful of rice for texture, this traditional Greek chicken soup is a full meal in a bowl.

SERVES: 4

Preparation time: 5 minutes
Cooking time: 3¼ hours (slow cooker)
1½ hours (stovetop)

1 x 2 lb 12 oz (1.2 kg) chicken
4 fresh or dried bay leaves
4 cloves garlic, bruised
1 onion, quartered
handful oregano leaves
zest of 1 lemon, peeled off in long strips
½ teaspoon black peppercorns
½ cup (3½ oz/100 g) long-grain rice
2 eggs
3 tablespoons (45 ml) lemon juice
chopped dill, to serve

IN THE SLOW COOKER

Put the chicken, bay leaves, garlic, onion, oregano, lemon zest, peppercorns and 10 cups (87 fl oz/2.5 L) of water in a slow cooker. Cut out a circle of parchment paper to fit the slow cooker and lay it directly on the surface of the liquid. Cook on high for 3 hours until the chicken is just cooked through. Turn off the slow cooker. Carefully remove the chicken and set aside until cool enough to handle. Strain the stock through a fine sieve, discarding the solids.

Cook the rice in a small saucepan of boiling water for 10 minutes until just cooked. Drain.

Return 6 cups (52 fl oz/1.5 L) of the stock to the slow cooker and turn on to high. Shred the chicken meat, discarding the skin and bones. Add the chicken to the slow cooker, along with the rice.

Whisk the eggs in a bowl, gradually adding the lemon juice. Whisk in a ladleful of the soup, then a second ladleful. Stir the egg mixture into the slow cooker, then cook for 10 minutes until the soup thickens slightly.

Season to taste with salt and pepper, then scatter with chopped dill to serve.

ON THE STOVETOP

Put the chicken, bay leaves, garlic, onion, oregano, lemon zest, peppercorns and 8 cups (70 fl oz/2 L) of water in a large saucepan. Bring to a boil over medium heat, then cover with a lid and reduce the heat to low. Cook for 45 minutes or until the chicken is cooked through. Carefully remove the chicken and set aside until cool enough to handle.

Meanwhile, strain the stock through a fine sieve into a clean pan, discarding the solids. Add the rice. Bring to a boil, then reduce the heat to low and simmer for 10 minutes until the rice is just cooked.

Shred the chicken meat, discarding the skin and bones, and return to the pan.

Whisk the eggs in a bowl, gradually adding the lemon juice. Whisk in a ladleful of the soup to combine, then a second ladleful. Stir the egg mixture into the soup and cook for 3 to 4 minutes until the soup thickens slightly, taking care not to allow the soup to boil.

Season to taste with salt and pepper, then scatter with chopped dill to serve.

BROWN RICE CONGEE WITH PORK AND SHRIMP

With a slow cooker, you can turn your congee into breakfast: Just omit the ground pork and shrimp and cook it overnight on low, then serve with boiled eggs in the morning. If you like, you could use ground chicken or cubed thigh fillets instead of the pork, or even a poached chicken breast for a more delicate congee. For a change, try this with scallops, fish or crabmeat in place of shrimp.

SERVES: 4

Preparation time: 10 minutes
Cooking time: 5 hours (slow cooker)
2¾ hours (stovetop)

1 cup (6½ oz/185 g) medium-grain brown rice, rinsed
7 ounces (200 g) ground pork
4 cups (35 fl oz/1 L) chicken stock
1 tablespoon (15 ml) Chinese rice wine
2 scallions, thinly sliced on an angle, white and green parts kept separate
2 cloves garlic, finely chopped
1 tablespoon (8 g) finely shredded ginger
1 teaspoon ground white pepper
1 teaspoon salt
12 raw shrimp, peeled, deveined, tails left intact
chopped peanuts, cilantro sprigs, sliced red chili, sesame oil and soy sauce, to serve

IN THE SLOW COOKER

Combine the rice and pork in the slow cooker, then add the stock, rice wine, the white parts of the spring onions, garlic, ginger, pepper, salt and 3 cups (26 fl oz/750 ml) of water. Cook on high for 5 hours or until the rice has broken down to a soupy consistency. Add the shrimp and cook for a further 5 minutes or until cooked through.

Serve with the green parts of the spring onions, peanuts, cilantro sprigs, sliced red chili, sesame oil and soy sauce.

ON THE STOVETOP

Combine the rice and pork in a large, heavy-based saucepan. Add the stock, rice wine, the white parts of the scallions, garlic, ginger, pepper, salt and 3 cups (26 fl oz/750 ml) of water. Bring to a boil, then reduce the heat to a simmer. Cover with a lid and cook for about 2½ hours until the rice has broken down to a soupy consistency, stirring occasionally so it doesn't stick to the bottom of the pan. Add a little more water if necessary. Finally, add the shrimp and cook for 5 minutes or until cooked through.

Serve with the green parts of the scallions, peanuts, cilantro sprigs, sliced red chili, sesame oil and soy sauce.

FARRO MINESTRONE

Farro is a nutty grain traditionally used in hearty Italian soups. You should be able to find it in health food shops and some supermarkets, but pearl barley or your favorite legume or pasta could happily be added in its place.

SERVES: 4

Preparation time: 15 minutes
Cooking time: 5½ hours (slow cooker)
50 minutes (stovetop)

1 tablespoon (15 ml) extra virgin olive oil
1 red onion, cut into ½ inch (1 cm) dice
4 cloves garlic, finely chopped
1 large carrot, cut into ½ inch (1 cm) dice
3 slices bacon, coarsely chopped
2 stalks celery, cut into ½ inch (1 cm) dice
⅔ cup (5 oz/140 g) farro, rinsed
4 cups (35 fl oz/1 L) chicken stock
2¾ oz (75 g) piece of parmesan,
    finely grated, rind reserved
1 large waxy potato, peeled, cut into
    ⅝ inch (1.5 cm) pieces
1 tablespoon (2 g) finely chopped sage
3 cups (8 oz/225 g) finely shredded cavolo nero
    (Tuscan kale) or savoy cabbage
1 large zucchini, cut into ½ inch (1 cm) dice
extra virgin olive oil, crusty bread and basil leaves,
    to serve

IN THE SLOW COOKER

Heat the oil in a large frying pan over medium–high heat. Cook the onion, garlic, carrot, bacon and celery for 5 minutes until slightly softened. Add the farro, and cook for 1 minute, stirring to coat. Transfer to the slow cooker, along with the stock, parmesan rind, potato, sage and 2 cups (17 fl oz/500 ml) of water. Cook on low for 5 hours until the farro is almost tender. Add the cavolo nero and zucchini and cook for a further 15 minutes until the farro and vegetables are tender. Season with salt and pepper.

Serve with the grated parmesan, extra virgin olive oil, crusty bread and basil leaves.

ON THE STOVETOP

Heat the oil in a large, heavy-based saucepan over medium–high heat. Cook the onion, garlic, carrot, bacon and celery for 5 minutes until slightly softened. Add the farro and cook for 1 minute, stirring to coat, then add the stock, 4 cups (35 fl oz/1 L) of water and the parmesan rind. Bring to a boil, then reduce the heat to a simmer and cook for 20 minutes. Add the potato and cook for a further 10 minutes, then add the sage, cavolo nero and zucchini. Cook for 5 minutes until the farro and vegetables are tender. Season with salt and pepper.

Serve with the grated parmesan, extra virgin olive oil, crusty bread and basil leaves.

MOROCCAN HARIRA SOUP

Traditionally eaten to break the fast during Ramadan, this Moroccan soup also makes the perfect winter warmer. It's typically made with lamb, but chicken thighs or stewing beef could be used as an alternative. As long as you remember to soak the chickpeas overnight, this soup practically makes itself. Feel free to omit the saffron.

SERVES 6

Preparation time: 5 minutes
Cooking time: 9 hours (slow cooker)
2 hours (stovetop)

2 tablespoons (30 ml) extra virgin olive oil
1 lb 2 oz (500 g) lamb chops, trimmed
1 large onion, finely chopped
2 stalks celery, cut into ½ inch (1 cm) pieces
2 teaspoons ground ginger
2 teaspoons ground cinnamon
2 teaspoons ground turmeric
large pinch saffron threads, soaked
   in 1 tablespoon (15 ml) hot water
large handful each cilantro and parsley, finely
   chopped, including stalks
2 cans (14 oz /400 g) chopped tomatoes
4 cups (35 fl oz/1 L) chicken stock
½ cup (2½ oz/75 g) dried chickpeas, soaked
   overnight, drained and rinsed
¼ cup (2 oz/55 g) dried green lentils, rinsed
2 tablespoons (30 ml) lemon juice

IN THE SLOW COOKER

Put the oil, lamb chops, onion, celery, ginger, cinnamon, turmeric, saffron with its soaking liquid, the stalks from the cilantro and parsley, tomatoes, stock, chickpeas, lentils and 1 cup (9 fl oz/250 ml) of water in the slow cooker. Season with salt, then cook on low for 9 hours until the meat and legumes are tender.

Stir in the lemon juice, chopped parsley and cilantro and check the seasoning.

ON THE STOVETOP

Heat 1 tablespoon (15 ml) of the oil in a large, heavy-based saucepan over medium–high heat. Add the lamb, season with salt and cook for 2 minutes on each side until browned. Remove and set aside.

Reduce the heat to medium and add the remaining oil, onion, celery, ginger, cinnamon, turmeric, saffron with its soaking liquid and the stalks from the parsley and cilantro. Cook for 3 to 5 minutes until the vegetables start to soften. Return the meat to the pan, along with the tomatoes, stock, chickpeas and 1 cup (9 fl oz/250 ml) of water and bring to a boil. Reduce the heat to low, cover with a lid and cook, stirring occasionally, for 1 hour. Add the lentils and cook for 45 minutes until the meat and legumes are tender.

Stir in the lemon juice, chopped parsley and cilantro and check the seasoning.

VIETNAMESE BEEF NOODLE SOUP

SERVES: 6

Preparation time: 15 minutes
Cooking time: 9 hours (slow cooker)
3 hours (stovetop)

1 whole garlic bulb
2½ inch (6 cm) piece ginger
2 white onions
2 cinnamon sticks
4 star anise
4 black cardamom pods
1 teaspoon fennel seeds
1 teaspoon black peppercorns
1 lb 2 oz (500 g) beef brisket
1 lb 2 oz (500 g) beef shin, cut into small pieces –
   ask the butcher to do this
2¼ ounces (60 g) brown sugar
½ cup (4 fl oz/125 ml) fish sauce
10½ ounces (300 g) beef sirloin, very thinly sliced
rice noodles, herbs, bean sprouts, lime wedges
   and red chili, to serve

IN THE SLOW COOKER

Roast the garlic, ginger and onions (all left
unpeeled) over an open flame for 10 minutes
until completely blackened. Alternatively, cook
under a hot grill (broiler) for about 15 minutes.
Transfer to a bowl and, when they are cool
enough to handle, peel and roughly chop.

Heat a small frying pan over medium heat and
toast the cinnamon, star anise, cardamom
pods, fennel seeds and peppercorns until
fragrant. Transfer to a small piece of muslin
and tie with string to make a pouch.

Put the beef brisket and shin, sugar, fish
sauce, garlic, ginger, onions, spice pouch,
1 tablespoon of salt and 8 cups (70 fl oz/2 L)
of water into the slow cooker. Cook on low
for 9 hours until the meat is tender. Remove
the beef brisket and shin and when it is cool
enough to handle, thinly slice the brisket and
shred the shin.

Strain the soup through a large fine sieve
lined with muslin. Place the sirloin in warmed
bowls, then pour over the hot stock. Serve
with noodles, herbs, bean sprouts, lime
wedges and chili.

ON THE STOVETOP

Roast the garlic, ginger and onions (all left
unpeeled) over an open flame for 10 minutes
until completely blackened. Alternatively, cook
under a hot grill (broiler) for about 15 minutes.
Transfer to a bowl and, when they are cool
enough to handle, peel and roughly chop.

Heat a small frying pan over medium heat and
toast the cinnamon, star anise, cardamom
pods, fennel seeds and peppercorns until
fragrant. Transfer to a small piece of muslin
and tie with string to make a pouch.

Put the beef brisket and shin, 1 tablespoon
of salt (18 g) and 10 cups (87 fl oz/2.5 L) of
water into a large heavy-based saucepan.
Bring to a boil, then reduce the heat to a
simmer and cook for 30 minutes, skimming
off any impurities that rise to the surface.

Add the sugar, fish sauce, garlic, ginger,
onions and spice pouch to the pan and return
to a simmer over medium heat. Reduce the
heat to a low, cover with a lid and cook for
2 hours until the meat is tender. Remove
the beef brisket and shin and when it is cool
enough to handle, thinly slice the brisket
and shred the shin.

Strain the soup through a large fine sieve
lined with muslin. Place the sirloin in warmed
bowls, then pour over the hot stock. Serve
with noodles, herbs, bean sprouts, lime
wedges and chili.

SWEET POTATO AND CARROT SOUP WITH CHEESY AGNOLOTTI

Dumpling wrappers are a great shortcut for making filled pasta. Look for them in supermarkets or Asian grocers. For a simpler version, just add some ready-made filled pasta to the soup and simmer until warmed through.

SERVES: 4

Preparation time: 20 minutes
Cooking time: 3¼ hours (slow cooker)
1¼ hours (stovetop)

1 tablespoon (15 ml) extra virgin olive oil
2 cloves garlic, finely chopped
1 red onion, finely chopped
1 lb 12 oz (800 g) sweet potato,
   cut into ¾ inch (2 cm) pieces
3 carrots, cut into ½ inch (1 cm) slices
4 cups (35 fl oz/1 L) chicken or vegetable stock
6 sprigs thyme, tied together with kitchen string
5½ ounces (150 g) feta, crumbled
5½ ounces (150 g) bocconcini, coarsely chopped
20 dumpling wrappers
mint leaves, to serve

IN THE SLOW COOKER

Heat the oil in a large saucepan over medium heat. Cook the garlic and onion for 5 minutes until softened. Transfer to the slow cooker, along with the potato, carrots, stock, thyme and 1 cup (9 fl oz/250 ml) of water. Cook on high for 3 hours until the vegetables are very tender. Remove the thyme and discard.

Meanwhile, combine the cheeses in a bowl. Place 2 teaspoons of the cheese filling onto one half of each dumpling wrapper. Wet your hands and run a fingertip around the edge of the wrappers, then fold to enclose the filling, ensuring there are no air pockets. Press along the edges with the back of a fork to seal.

Bring a large saucepan of salted water to a boil. Cook the agnolotti for 2 minutes until they float to the surface, then drain.

Remove one-third of the soup and purée with a stick blender, food processor or blender until smooth. Return to the slow cooker, along with the agnolotti, and cook for about 5 minutes until warmed through.

Season the soup, then serve with mint leaves.

ON THE STOVETOP

Heat the oil in a large saucepan over medium heat. Cook the garlic and onion for 5 minutes until softened. Add the potato, carrots, stock and thyme, 2 cups (17 fl oz/500 ml) of water and bring to a boil over medium heat. Reduce the heat to low, cover with a lid and cook for 1 hour until the vegetables are very tender. Remove the thyme and discard.

Meanwhile, combine the cheeses in a bowl. Place 2 teaspoons of the cheese filling onto one half of each dumpling wrapper. Wet your hands and run a fingertip around the edge of the wrappers, then fold to enclose the filling, ensuring there are no air pockets. Press along the edges with the back of a fork to seal.

Bring a large saucepan of salted water to a boil. Cook the agnolotti for 2 minutes until they float to the surface, then drain.

Remove one-third of the soup and purée with a stick blender, food processor or blender until smooth. Return to the slow cooker, along with the agnolotti, and cook for about 5 minutes until warmed through.

Season the soup, then serve with mint leaves.

CHICKEN AND SWEET CORN SOUP

A classic combination of sweet golden corn and tender shredded chicken breast, given a twist with the aniseed flavor of tarragon. For a smoother soup, pulse half of the corn kernels in a food processor before adding to the soup.

SERVES: 4

Preparation time: 5 minutes
Cooking time: 3 hours (slow cooker)
35 minutes (stovetop)

1 tablespoon (15 ml) olive oil
1 leek, white and pale green parts only,
   halved lengthwise then thinly sliced
2 cloves garlic, finely chopped
1 stalk celery, cut into ½ inch (1 cm) pieces
½ cup (4 fl oz/125 ml) dry white wine
4 cobs corn, kernels cut from the cobs
1 potato, such as desiree or dutch cream,
   cut into ⅝ inch (1.5 cm) pieces
4 cups (35 fl oz/1 L) chicken stock
2 tablespoons (8 g) coarsely chopped tarragon
2 chicken breast fillets

IN THE SLOW COOKER

Put the oil, leek, garlic, celery, wine, corn, potato, stock, half of the tarragon and 2 cups (17 fl oz/500 ml) of water into the slow cooker. Season with salt and pepper, then cook on high for 2½ to 3 hours until the potato is just tender. Turn the slow cooker down to low, add the chicken and cook for 20 to 30 minutes until cooked through.

Remove the chicken from the slow cooker. Once it is cool enough to handle, shred the meat and return to the slow cooker for about 5 minutes to warm through.

Serve the soup scattered with the rest of the tarragon.

ON THE STOVETOP

Heat the oil in a large, heavy-based saucepan over medium heat. Cook the leek and celery for 3 minutes until translucent, then add the garlic and cook for a minute until fragrant. Add the wine and let it boil for 3 minutes to evaporate the alcohol.

Add the potato, stock, half of the tarragon, corn and 2 cups (17 fl oz/500 ml) of water. Season with salt and pepper. Bring to a boil, then reduce the heat to a simmer and cook for 5 minutes. Add the chicken, cover with a lid and cook for 10 minutes until the chicken is cooked through and the potato is tender.

Remove the chicken from the pan. Once it is cool enough to handle, shred the meat and return to the pan for about 5 minutes to warm through.

Serve the soup scattered with the rest of the tarragon.

SEAFOOD CHOWDER

A rich and creamy chowder is hard to beat. Serve with crusty bread and perhaps a salad for a soothing supper. You can mix up the seafood, according to what looks good on the day: You could use mussels instead of clams, or try fish and shrimp.

SERVES: 4

Preparation time: 5 minutes + 1 hour soaking
Cooking time: 2¾ hours (slow cooker)
15 minutes (stovetop)

16 clams, soaked for 1 hour,
  drained and rinsed
3 tablespoons (40 g) butter
1 leek, white parts only, halved lengthwise
  then thinly sliced
2 cloves garlic, finely chopped
1 slice bacon, cut into strips
1 tablespoon (8 g) cornstarch
4 cups (35 fl oz/1 L) fish or seafood stock
1 fresh or dried bay leaf
4 sprigs lemon thyme or thyme, leaves picked
pinch cayenne pepper
2 cups (17 fl oz/500 ml) milk
5½ ounces (150 g) skinless hot-smoked salmon
  fillet, flaked into large pieces
12 scallops
chopped parsley, extra virgin olive oil and
  crusty bread, to serve

IN THE SLOW COOKER

Heat a large frying pan over medium–high heat. Add the clams and cover with a lid. Cook for 1 minute until the shells have just opened. Transfer to a bowl and set aside.

Reduce the heat to medium and add the butter to the pan. Cook the leek, garlic and bacon for 4 minutes until lightly golden, then sprinkle in the flour and cook for 1 minute, stirring. Gradually stir in the stock, then add the bay leaf, thyme and cayenne pepper.

Season with salt and pepper, then transfer to the slow cooker. Cook on high for 2 hours, then turn the slow cooker down to low. Stir in the milk and add the salmon, scallops and the clams with any juices. Cook for 30 minutes until the fish and seafood is cooked through.

Serve with chopped parsley, extra virgin olive oil and crusty bread.

ON THE STOVETOP

Heat the butter in a large frying pan over medium–high heat. Cook the leek, garlic and bacon for 4 minutes until lightly golden, then sprinkle in the flour and cook for 1 minute, stirring. Gradually stir in the stock, then add the bay leaf, thyme and cayenne pepper.

Bring to a boil, add the clams and cover with a lid. Cook for 1 to 2 minutes until they start to open. Add the milk and bring to just below a simmer. Add the salmon and scallops and cook for 2 minutes until the seafood is just cooked through and the clams have opened. Season with salt and pepper.

Serve with chopped parsley, extra virgin olive oil and crusty bread.

SHRIMP AND SQUID LAKSA

SERVES: 4

Preparation time: 25 minutes
Cooking time: 3½ hours (slow cooker)
1¼ hours (stovetop)

3 tablespoons (45 ml) grapeseed or rice bran oil
12 raw shrimp, peeled, deveined, tails left intact,
    heads and shells reserved
2 cans (9½ fl oz/ 270 ml) coconut milk
2 cups (17 fl oz/500 ml) chicken stock
1 lb 2 oz (500 g) squid tubes, cut into bite-sized
    pieces, scored
14 ounces (400 g) vermicelli noodles
handful broccolini, cut into 2 inch (5 cm) lengths
5½ ounces (150 g) tofu puffs, halved diagonally
    –optional
bean sprouts, cilantro sprigs, Vietnamese mint
    (laksa) leaves, crispy fried shallots and lime
    wedges, to serve

Laksa paste

1 tablespoon (8 g) finely chopped galangal or
    ginger
1 stem lemongrass, tough outer stems removed,
    white part only, chopped
4 long red chilies, coarsely chopped
4 cloves garlic, coarsely chopped
1 tablespoon finely grated fresh turmeric
    or 2 teaspoons ground turmeric
6 red shallots, coarsely chopped
2 tablespoons macadamia nuts, coarsely grated
¾ ounce (20 g) belacan (shrimp paste), wrapped in
    foil and toasted in a dry frying pan until fragrant
1 tablespoon ground coriander
1 ounce (30 g) palm sugar, coarsely grated,
    or brown sugar

IN THE SLOW COOKER

To make the laksa paste, process all the
ingredients in a food processor until smooth.

Heat the oil in a large frying pan over high
heat. Cook the shrimp heads and shells for
5 minutes until they turn red, pushing down
on them with the back of a wooden spoon.
Remove with a slotted spoon and discard.
Reduce the heat to medium, add the laksa
paste and cook for 6 to 8 minutes until

fragrant, stirring regularly. Stir in the coconut
milk and cook for 3 minutes until the oil
separates. Transfer to the slow cooker, along
with the stock, squid and 2 cups (17 fl oz/
500 ml) of water. Cook on low for 3 hours.

Meanwhile, prepare the noodles according
to the packet instructions.

Add the shrimp, broccolini and tofu puffs,
if using, to the slow cooker and cook for a
further 10 to 15 minutes until cooked through.

Serve with the noodles, bean sprouts, cilantro
sprigs, Vietnamese mint, crispy fried shallots
and lime wedges.

ON THE STOVETOP

To make the laksa paste, process all the
ingredients in a food processor until smooth.

Heat the oil in a large frying pan over high heat.
Cook the shrimp heads and shells for 5 minutes
until they turn red, pushing down on them with
the back of a wooden spoon. Remove with a
slotted spoon and discard. Reduce the heat to
medium, add the laksa paste and cook for
6 to 8 minutes until fragrant, stirring regularly.
Stir in the coconut milk and cook for 3 minutes
until the oil separates. Add the stock and
3 cups (26 fl oz/750 ml) of water. Bring to a
boil, then reduce the heat to low. Add the squid
and cook for 45 minutes until tender. Add more
water if necessary.

Meanwhile, prepare the noodles according
to the packet instructions.

Add the shrimp, broccolini and tofu puffs,
if using, to the pan and cook for 5 minutes
until cooked through.

Serve with the noodles, bean sprouts, cilantro
sprigs, Vietnamese mint, crispy fried shallots
and lime wedges.

TORTILLA SOUP WITH SHREDDED CHICKEN

The deep smoky flavor of this soup comes from chipotle chilies in adobo sauce. These are sold in small containers at specialty food shops and delicatessens; if you can't find any, just add 3 teaspoons of smoked paprika and 2 chopped fresh chilies instead.

SERVES: 4

Preparation time: 5 minutes
Cooking time: 5 hours (slow cooker)
1 hour (stovetop)

½ cup (4 fl oz/125 ml) rice bran or grapeseed oil
1 onion, finely chopped
4 cloves garlic, finely chopped
2 teaspoons ground paprika
1 teaspoon ground cumin
1 teaspoon ground coriander
2 chipotle chilies in adobo sauce, finely chopped
1 can (14 ounces/400 g) chopped tomatoes
4 cups (35 fl oz/1 L) chicken stock
2 chicken breast fillets
2 corn tortillas, halved, cut into ½ inch (1 cm) strips
cilantro sprigs, diced avocado, lime wedges,
    crumbled fresh cheese or feta, to serve

IN THE SLOW COOKER

Heat 1 tablespoon (15 ml) of the oil in a large frying pan over medium heat. Cook the onion, garlic, paprika, cumin and coriander for 5 minutes until slightly softened. Transfer to the slow cooker, along with the chilies, tomatoes and stock. Season with salt and pepper, then cook on low for 4 hours. Add the chicken breasts and cook for a further 40 minutes until cooked through, then remove and set aside until cool enough to handle.

Meanwhile, heat the remaining oil in the frying pan over medium heat. Fry the tortilla strips for 6 to 8 minutes until light golden and crisp. Remove, drain well on paper towel and season with salt.

Using an immersion blender, food processor or blender, purée the soup until smooth. Check the seasoning.

Shred the chicken with two forks, then return to the slow cooker and cook for a further 5 minutes to warm though.

Serve with tortilla strips, cilantro sprigs, diced avocado, lime wedges and cheese.

ON THE STOVETOP

Heat 1 tablespoon (15 ml) of the oil in a large saucepan over medium heat. Cook the onion, garlic, paprika, cumin and coriander for about 5 minutes until the onion and garlic soften slightly. Add the chilies, tomatoes and stock and season with salt and pepper. Bring to a boil, then reduce the heat to a simmer and cook for 30 minutes. Add the chicken breasts and cook for 20 to 30 minutes until cooked through, then remove and set aside until cool enough to handle.

Meanwhile, heat the remaining oil in a frying pan over medium heat. Fry the tortilla strips for 6 to 8 minutes until light golden and crisp. Remove, drain well on paper towel and season with salt.

Using an immersion blender, food processor or blender, purée the soup until smooth. Check the seasoning.

Shred the chicken with two forks, then return to the pan. Cook for a further 5 minutes until warmed though.

Serve with tortilla strips, cilantro sprigs, diced avocado, lime wedges and cheese.

CAULIFLOWER AND CANNELLINI BEAN SOUP WITH PANCETTA

For this velvety soup, you can use any white beans that are roughly the same size as cannellini beans, such as great northern. Just don't forget to soak them over-night. Celeriac makes a great winter-time substitute for the cauliflower.

SERVES: 4

Preparation time: 5 minutes + overnight soaking
Cooking time: 4½ hours (slow cooker)
2¼ hours (stovetop)

2 tablespoons (30 ml) extra virgin olive oil,
   plus extra to serve
12 pancetta slices
handful sage leaves
2 cloves garlic, coarsely chopped
1 onion, finely chopped
1 cup (7 oz/200 g) dried cannellini beans,
   soaked overnight, drained and rinsed
1 small head cauliflower, broken into florets,
   stem thickly sliced
5 cups (44 fl oz/1.25 L) chicken stock

IN THE SLOW COOKER

Heat 1 tablespoon (15 ml) of the oil in a large, heavy-based saucepan over medium–high heat and cook the pancetta for 2 minutes. Turn the pancetta, then add the sage leaves to the pan and cook for 2 minutes until crisp. Remove the pancetta and sage and set aside. (You may need to do this in batches, depending on the size of your pan.)

Add the remaining oil to the pan and cook the garlic and onion for 3 minutes until lightly golden. Add the beans and 1½ cups (13 fl oz/ 375 ml) of water. Bring to a boil and cook for 20 minutes, then transfer to the slow cooker, along with the cauliflower and stock. Cook on high for 4 hours until the cauliflower and beans are tender.

Using a blender or food processor, purée the soup until smooth. Check the seasoning.

Serve with the crispy pancetta and sage.

ON THE STOVETOP

Heat 1 tablespoon (15 ml) of the oil in a large, heavy-based saucepan over medium–high heat and cook the pancetta for 2 minutes. Turn the pancetta, then add the sage leaves to the pan and cook for 2 minutes until crisp. Remove the pancetta and sage and set aside. (You may need to do this in batches, depending on the size of your pan.)

Add the remaining oil to the pan and cook the garlic and onion for 3 minutes until lightly golden. Add the beans and 3 cups (26 fl oz/ 750 ml) of water. Bring to a boil and cook for 30 minutes, then add the cauliflower and stock and return to a boil. Cover with a lid, reduce to a simmer and cook for 1½ hours until the beans and cauliflower are tender.

Using a blender or food processor, purée the soup until smooth. Check the seasoning.

Serve with the crispy pancetta and sage.

stews

&

casseroles

HARISSA LAMB TAGINE WITH APRICOTS

The warmth of sweet spices and apricots mellow the richness of lamb to make this a real treat, especially with the crunch of toasted almonds and sesame seeds. All it needs is a large mound of fluffy couscous. This simple tagine would work just as well with lamb shoulder or leg instead of neck fillet.

SERVES: 4

Preparation time: 5 minutes
Cooking time: 7¼ hours (slow cooker)
2 hours 20 minutes (stovetop)

1 tablespoon (15 ml) olive oil
2 lb 4 oz (1 kg) lamb neck fillet,
    cut into 1¼ inch (3 cm) cubes
1½ tablespoons (20 g) butter
½ teaspoon ground ginger
½ teaspoon ground cinnamon
1 onion, halved, thinly sliced
handful cilantro, roots cleaned and finely
    chopped, leaves coarsely chopped
pinch saffron threads, soaked in 2 teaspoons
    hot water
7 oz (200 g) dried apricots
2 tablespoons (30 g) harissa paste
½ cup (2¾ oz/80 g) blanched almonds, toasted
couscous and toasted sesame seeds, to serve

IN THE SLOW COOKER

Heat the oil in a frying pan over medium–high heat. Season the lamb with salt and pepper. In batches, cook the lamb for 5 minutes until browned. Transfer to the slow cooker.

Reduce the heat to medium and add the butter, ginger, cinnamon, onion and cilantro roots. Cook for 3 minutes until the onion is slightly softened. Transfer to the slow cooker. Stir in the saffron and its soaking liquid, along with the apricots, harissa paste and ½ cup (4 fl oz/125 ml) of water. Cook on low for 7 hours until the meat is tender. Stir in the cilantro leaves and almonds, then serve with couscous and sesame seeds.

ON THE STOVETOP

Heat the oil in a large, heavy-based saucepan over medium–high heat. Season the lamb with salt and pepper. In batches, cook the lamb for 5 minutes until browned. Remove and set aside.

Reduce the heat to medium and add the butter, ginger, cinnamon, onion and cilantro roots. Cook for 3 minutes until the onion is slightly softened. Stir in the saffron and its soaking liquid, along with the apricots, harissa and lamb and 1 cup (9 fl oz/250 ml) of water. Bring to a boil, then reduce the heat to low. Cover with a lid and simmer for about 2 hours until the meat is tender, stirring occasionally. Stir in the cilantro leaves and almonds, then serve with couscous and sesame seeds.

CHOUCROUTE

You can use other cuts of pork, such as hock, and any good-quality pork sausages to make this robust dish from the Alsace region of France.

SERVES: 4

Preparation time: 10 minutes
Cooking time: 4¼ hours (slow cooker)
4¼ hours (oven)

1 tablespoon (15 ml) olive oil
9 ounces (250 g) speck or bacon, cut into strips
2 lb 4 oz (1 kg) sauerkraut, rinsed and squeezed dry
1 green apple, peeled, coarsely grated
1 onion, finely chopped
4 cloves garlic, finely chopped
8 baby or new potatoes, halved
14 ounces (400 g) pork shoulder meat,
    cut into ½ inch (1 cm) slices
2 bratwurst sausages, thickly sliced
6 cloves
12 juniper berries
2 fresh or dried bay leaves
1½ cups (13 fl oz/375 ml) white wine,
    such as riesling
mustard and rye bread, to serve

IN THE SLOW COOKER

Heat the oil in a frying pan over medium heat and cook the speck for 4 minutes until golden. Transfer to a bowl and combine with the sauerkraut and apple.

Add the onion and garlic to the pan and cook for 4 minutes until softened. Transfer to the bowl with the sauerkraut and mix well.

Add half of the sauerkraut mixture to the slow cooker, together with the potatoes, and spread out evenly. Arrange the pork and sausages over the top. Scatter with 3 cloves, 6 juniper berries and 1 bay leaf. Season with salt and pepper. Top with the remaining sauerkraut mixture, then scatter with the remaining cloves, juniper berries and bay leaf. Season with salt and pepper, then pour in the wine and cook on high for 4 hours until the meat is tender.

Serve with mustard and rye bread.

IN THE OVEN

Preheat the oven to 235°F/gas mark ½ (120°C).

Heat the oil in a large flameproof casserole over medium heat and cook the speck for 4 minutes until golden. Transfer to a bowl and combine with the sauerkraut and apple.

Add the onion and garlic to the pan and cook for 4 minutes until softened. Transfer to the bowl with the sauerkraut and mix to combine.

Add half of the sauerkraut mixture to the pan, together with the potatoes, and spread out evenly. Arrange the pork and sausages over the top. Scatter with 3 cloves, 6 juniper berries and 1 bay leaf. Season with salt and pepper. Top with the remaining sauerkraut mixture, then scatter with the remaining cloves, juniper berries and bay leaf. Season with salt and pepper, then pour in the wine and bake in the oven for 4 hours until the meat is tender.

Serve with mustard and rye bread.

SPANISH OXTAIL AND CHORIZO STEW

Serve this unctuous meaty stew with plenty of white bean or mashed potatoes to soak up the sauce. To make white bean mash, cook your favorite white beans until they are very tender, then mash or blend with a generous amount of olive oil and salt and pepper. Other cuts of beef that would work here include short rib or shin.

SERVES: 4–6

Preparation time: 10 minutes
Cooking time: 9½ hours (slow cooker)
3½ hours (oven)

½ cup (2¾ oz/75 g) all-purpose flour
4 lb 8 oz (2 kg) oxtail, cut into 2 inch (5 cm)
  pieces – ask the butcher to do this
3 tablespoons (45 ml) olive oil
1 onion, finely chopped
2 cloves garlic, finely chopped
2 carrots, coarsely chopped
2 cups (17 fl oz/500 ml) white wine
2 cups (17 fl oz/500 ml) chicken stock
2 chorizo sausages, coarsely chopped
2 teaspoons smoked paprika
finely grated zest and juice of 1 orange
2 sprigs rosemary, leaves picked
2 cans (14 ounces/400 g) tomatoes
parsley leaves, to serve

IN THE SLOW COOKER

Put the flour in a bowl and season with salt and pepper. Dust the oxtail in the flour, shaking off any excess. Heat 1 tablespoon (15 ml) of the oil in a large frying pan over medium–high heat. Cook half of the oxtail for 6 minutes, turning to brown evenly. Drain well on paper towel. Repeat with another tablespoon (15 ml) of oil and the other half of the oxtail.

Reduce the heat to medium and add the remaining oil to the pan. Cook the onion, garlic and carrots for 5 minutes until the onion is translucent. Add the wine to the pan and let it boil for 5 minutes to evaporate the alcohol. Transfer to the slow cooker, along with all the remaining ingredients except the parsley. Stir well, then add the oxtail and cook on low for 9 hours until the oxtail is falling off the bone. Skim any fat from the surface.

Scatter with parsley leaves, then serve.

IN THE OVEN

Preheat the oven to 300°F/gas mark 2 (150°C).

Put the flour in a bowl and season with salt and pepper. Dust the oxtail in the flour, shaking off any excess. Heat 1 tablespoon (15 ml) of the oil in a large lidded flameproof casserole over medium–high heat. Cook half of the oxtail for 6 minutes, turning to brown evenly. Drain well on paper towel. Repeat with another tablespoon (15 ml) of oil and the other half of the oxtail.

Reduce the heat to medium and add the remaining oil to the pan. Cook the onion, garlic and carrots for 5 minutes until the onion is translucent. Add the wine to the pan and let it boil for 5 minutes to evaporate the alcohol. Add all the remaining ingredients except the parsley and stir well. Cut out a circle of parchment paper to fit the casserole and lay it directly on the surface of the liquid. Cover with a lid and cook in the oven for 3 hours, turning the oxtail halfway through. Skim any fat from the surface.

Scatter with parsley, then serve.

BEEF AND GUINNESS STEW WITH BUTTERMILK DUMPLINGS

SERVES: 4

Preparation time: 20 minutes
Cooking time: 8½ hours (slow cooker)
3 hours (stovetop)

⅓ cup (1¾ oz/50 g) all-purpose flour
2 lb 4 oz (1 kg) beef cheeks,
    cut into 1½ inch (4 cm) cubes
3 tablespoons (45 ml) olive oil
1 onion, finely chopped
1 clove garlic, finely chopped
3 tablespoons (45 ml) tomato paste
1 carrot, cut into ¾ inch (2 cm) cubes
1 fresh or dried bay leaf
1 teaspoon finely chopped rosemary
1 cup (9 fl oz/250 ml) Guinness
2 teaspoons raw sugar
1 cup (9 fl oz/250 ml) beef stock

Buttermilk dumplings
1 cup (5½ oz/150 g) self-rising flour
3½ tablespoons (1½ oz/40 g) cold butter, cubed
3 tablespoons (15 g) finely grated parmesan
1 tablespoon (4 g) chopped parsley, plus extra to
    serve
½ cup (4 fl oz/125 ml) buttermilk
1 egg, lightly beaten

IN THE SLOW COOKER

Put the flour into a bowl and season well with salt and pepper. Dust the beef in the seasoned flour, shaking off any excess.

Heat 1 tablespoon (15 ml) of the oil in a large frying pan over high heat. In batches, cook the beef for 5 minutes until browned, then transfer to the slow cooker. Reduce the heat to medium and add the remaining oil to the pan. Cook the onion and garlic for 3 minutes until lightly golden. Add the tomato paste and cook for a minute, then add the carrot, bay leaf, rosemary, Guinness and sugar. Season with salt and pepper, then let it boil for 5 minutes to evaporate the alcohol. Transfer to the slow cooker, along with the stock. Cook on low for 7 hours. Turn the slow cooker up to high.

For the buttermilk dumplings, put the flour into a large bowl. Rub the butter into the flour until it resembles coarse breadcrumbs. Mix in the parmesan and parsley, then the buttermilk and egg, to make a sticky dough.

Drop 12 heaping tablespoons of the dumpling dough on top of the stew and cover with the lid. Cook for 1 hour until the dumplings are cooked through. Serve with parsley.

ON THE STOVETOP

Put the flour into a bowl and season well with salt and pepper. Dust the beef in the seasoned flour, shaking off any excess.

Heat 1 tablespoon (15 ml) of the oil in a large, heavy-based saucepan over high heat. In batches, cook the beef for 5 minutes until browned. Remove and set aside. Reduce the heat to medium and add the remaining oil to the pan. Cook the onion and garlic for 3 minutes until lightly golden. Add the tomato paste and cook for a minute, then add the carrot, bay leaf, rosemary, Guinness and sugar. Let it boil for 5 minutes to evaporate the alcohol, then pour in the stock and 1 cup (9 fl oz/250 ml) of water. Season with salt and pepper, then bring to a simmer. Reduce the heat to low and cover with a lid. Simmer for 2 to 2½ hours until the beef is almost tender.

For the buttermilk dumplings, put the flour into a large bowl. Rub the butter into the flour until it resembles coarse breadcrumbs. Mix in the parmesan and parsley, then the buttermilk and egg, to make a sticky dough.

Drop 12 heaping tablespoons of the dumpling dough on top of the stew, and cover with a lid. Cook for 30 minutes until the dumplings are cooked through. Serve with parsley.

PORK, APPLE AND CIDER PIE

SERVES: 4

Preparation time: 10 minutes
Cooking time: 6½ hours (slow cooker)
2 hours (oven)

3 tablespoons (25 g) cornstarch
2 lb 4 oz (1 kg) pork shoulder meat,
    cut into 1¼ inch (3 cm) cubes
3 tablespoons (45 ml) olive oil
1 red onion, finely chopped
2 cloves garlic, finely chopped
2 tablespoons (5 g) finely chopped sage
1 teaspoon fennel seeds, coarsely ground
1⅓ cups (10¼ fl oz/330 ml) apple cider
2 granny smith apples, peeled, cored,
    cut into 1¼ inch (3 cm) cubes
2 lb 4 oz (1 kg) desiree potatoes, peeled,
    cut into 1½ inch (4 cm) cubes
3½ tablespoons (1¾ oz/50 g) butter
3 tablespoons (45 ml) milk
chopped parsley, to serve

IN THE SLOW COOKER

Put the cornstarch into a bowl and season well with salt and pepper. Coat the pork in the seasoned flour.

Heat 1 tablespoon (15 ml) of the oil in a large frying pan over high heat and cook the pork for about 5 minutes or until browned. Transfer to the slow cooker. Reduce the heat to medium, add the onion, garlic, sage and fennel and cook for 2 minutes or until softened. Add the cider and let it boil for 1 to 2 minutes to evaporate the alcohol. Transfer to the slow cooker, along with the apples, and mix. Season well with salt and pepper, then cook on low for 6 hours until the pork is tender.

Meanwhile, put the potatoes in a large saucepan of cold salted water. Bring to a boil and cook for 12 minutes until tender. Drain and mash with a potato masher. Add the butter and milk and mix well.

Spoon the potato onto the surface of the pork and apple mixture, making a scalloped pattern with the back of the spoon, if you like. Cook for a further 15 minutes or until warmed through.

Serve with chopped parsley.

IN THE OVEN

Preheat the oven to 315°F/gas mark 2–3 (160°C).

Put the cornstarch into a bowl and season well with salt and pepper. Coat the pork in the seasoned flour.

Heat 1 tablespoon (15 ml) of the oil in a large frying pan over high heat and cook the pork for about 5 minutes or until browned. Remove and set aside. Reduce the heat to medium, add the onion, garlic, sage and fennel and cook for 2 minutes or until softened. Return the pork to the pan, pour in the cider and let it boil for 1 to 2 minutes to evaporate the alcohol. Transfer to a 10 cups (87 fl oz/2.5 L) baking dish, along with the apples, and mix to combine. Season well with salt and pepper, then cover tightly with foil and bake for 1½ hours until the pork is tender.

Meanwhile, put the potatoes in a large saucepan of cold salted water. Bring to a boil and cook for 12 minutes until tender. Drain and mash with a potato masher. Add the butter and milk and mix well.

Increase the oven temperature to 375°F/gas mark 5 (190°C). Spoon the potato onto the surface of the pork and apple mixture, making a scalloped pattern with the back of the spoon, if you like. Bake for 15 minutes until warmed through and lightly golden.

Serve with chopped parsley.

MEDITERRANEAN STUFFED SQUID

Packed with sunny flavors, this squid is the perfect farewell to the winter months. If you want a change from bread and salad, orzo makes a great accompaniment.

SERVES: 4

Preparation time: 20 minutes + cooling time
Cooking time: 3¾ hours (slow cooker)
1¼ hours (oven)

1 tablespoon (15 ml) olive oil
2 lb 4 oz (1 kg) small squid or calamari, cleaned, tentacles reserved and finely chopped
1 chorizo, casing removed, finely chopped
2 cloves garlic, finely chopped
10½ ounces (300 g) fennel, finely chopped
4 tablespoons (50 g) long-grain rice
1 cup (9 fl oz/250 ml) white wine
½ teaspoon finely grated lemon zest
2¾ ounces (75 g) feta cheese, crumbled
1½ tablespoons (6 g) finely chopped dill
3 cups (26 fl oz/750 ml) fish stock
crusty bread, lemon slices and tomato salad, to serve

IN THE SLOW COOKER

Heat the oil in a large frying pan over medium heat. Add the squid tentacles, chorizo, garlic and fennel and cook for 5 minutes until the fennel has softened. Add the rice and cook for a further minute, just to coat the grains. Add the wine and let it boil for 6 to 8 minutes to evaporate the alcohol. Set aside to cool completely.

When the fennel mixture is cool, stir in the lemon zest, feta and dill. Season with salt and pepper, then stuff the squid bodies with the mixture. Put the stuffed squid into the slow cooker and cover with the stock. Cook on low for 3½ hours until the squid is tender.

Serve with crusty bread, lemon slices and tomato salad.

IN THE OVEN

Heat the oil in a large, flameproof casserole over medium heat. Add the squid tentacles, chorizo, garlic and fennel and cook for about 5 minutes until the fennel has softened. Add the rice and cook for a further minute, just to coat the grains. Add the wine and let it boil for 6 to 8 minutes to evaporate the alcohol. Set aside to cool completely.

Preheat the oven to 300°F/gas mark 2 (150°C).

When the fennel mixture is cool, stir in the lemon zest, feta and dill. Season with salt and pepper, then stuff the squid bodies with the mixture. Put the stuffed squid into the casserole and cover with the stock. Cut out a circle of parchment paper to fit the casserole and lay it directly on the surface of the liquid. Cook in the oven for 1 hour until the squid is tender.

Serve with crusty bread, lemon slices and tomato salad.

JERK CHICKEN

Slow cooking rather than barbecuing this Jamaican classic makes the chicken meltingly tender. It's usually heavily heated up with chilies, so increase or decrease to your liking. Two of each type of chili is a good halfway point.

SERVES: 4

Preparation time: 20 minutes
(+ 1 hour marinating if cooking in oven)
Cooking time: 7 hours (slow cooker)
1½ hours (oven)

1 onion, coarsely chopped
6 spring onions (scallions), coarsely chopped
4 cloves garlic, coarsely chopped
2 to 4 habanero or jalapeño chilies (or a mixture), seeds removed, coarsely chopped
2 tablespoons (5 g) thyme leaves
2 teaspoons salt
2 teaspoons cracked black pepper
2 tablespoons (12 g) ground allspice
2 teaspoons ground ginger
2 teaspoons ground cinnamon
2 teaspoons raw sugar
½ cup (4 fl oz/125 ml) lime juice
8 chicken thighs
2 tablespoons (30 ml) grapeseed or rice bran oil
steamed rice and kidney beans, corn, scallions and lime wedges, to serve

IN THE SLOW COOKER

Pulse the onion, spring onions, garlic, chilies, thyme, salt, pepper, allspice, ginger, cinnamon, sugar and lime juice in a food processor or blender until smooth. Put the chicken into the slow cooker, add the marinade and mix to coat.

Heat the oil in a large frying over medium–high heat. Sear the chicken for 2 minutes on each side until browned.

Return the chicken and any pan juices to the slow cooker, along with 1 cup (9 fl oz/250 ml) of water. Cook on low for 7 hours.

Serve with steamed rice and kidney beans, corn, scallions and lime wedges.

IN THE OVEN

Pulse the onion, spring onions, garlic, chilies, thyme, salt, pepper, allspice, ginger, cinnamon, sugar and lime juice in a food processor or blender until smooth. Transfer to a large bowl and add the chicken. Mix well, then cover and leave to marinate in the fridge for 1 hour.

Preheat the oven to 375°F/gas mark 5 (190°C).

Heat the oil in a large, heavy-based roasting pan over medium–high heat. Remove the chicken from the marinade (reserving the marinade) and sear for 2 minutes on each side until browned. Remove from the heat and turn the chicken skin-side up, then pour in the reserved marinade and 2 cups (17 fl oz/500 ml) of water. Cook in the oven for 15 minutes, then reduce the temperature to 235°F/gas mark ½ (120°C) and cook for another hour until the chicken is cooked through.

Serve with steamed rice and kidney beans, corn, scallions and lime wedges.

BEEF SHORT RIB POUTINE

This hugely popular Canadian invention is the ultimate comfort dish. You could use chuck steak or beef shin as a substitute or omit the meat altogether and replace the beef and chicken stocks with vegetable stock to make it vegetarian.

SERVES: 4–6

Preparation time: 15 minutes
Cooking time: 8½ hours (slow cooker)
3 hours (oven)

5 medium waxy potatoes, cut into wedges
1 tablespoon (15 ml) olive oil
2 lb 4 oz (1 kg) beef short rib, cut into single ribs
3 tablespoons (1½ oz/40 g) butter
1 red onion, finely chopped
2 cloves garlic, finely chopped
3 tablespoons (20 g) all-purpose flour
2 cups (17 fl oz/500 ml) chicken stock
1 cup (9 fl oz/250 ml) beef stock
1 tablespoon (15 ml) Worcestershire sauce
6 sprigs thyme, tied together with string
7 ounces (200 g) melting cheese, such as
   provolone, raclette or mozzarella
chopped parsley or chives, to serve

IN THE SLOW COOKER

Arrange the potatoes in the base of the slow cooker in a single layer.

Heat the oil in a large frying pan over medium–high heat. Season the beef with salt and cook for 5 minutes until browned, then transfer to the slow cooker.

Reduce the heat to medium and add the butter to the pan. Cook the onion and garlic for 3 minutes until lightly golden, then sprinkle in the flour and cook for a minute, stirring. Gradually stir in both stocks, then bring to a boil and add the Worcestershire sauce and thyme sprigs. Pour into the slow cooker and cook on low for 6 hours. Remove the beef and roughly shred, then return to the slow cooker and cook for another 2 hours. Remove the thyme and discard.

Add the cheese to the slow cooker and cook for a further 15 minutes until melted.

Serve with chopped parsley or chives.

IN THE OVEN

Preheat the oven to 325°F/gas mark 3 (170°C). Heat the oil in a large, flameproof casserole over medium–high heat. Season the beef with salt and cook for 5 minutes until browned, then remove and set aside.

Reduce the heat to medium and melt the butter in the pan. Cook the onion and garlic for 3 minutes until lightly golden, then sprinkle in the flour and cook for a minute, stirring. Gradually stir in both stocks, along with 1 cup (9 fl oz/250 ml) of water, and bring to a boil. Add the Worcestershire sauce and thyme, then return the beef to the casserole and cook in the oven for 2 hours. Remove the beef and roughly shred, then return to the casserole, together with the potatoes. Cook for 45 minutes until the beef and potatoes are tender. Remove the thyme and discard.

Scatter the pan with the cheese and return to the oven for 5 to 10 minutes until melted.

Serve with chopped parsley or chives.

VEAL STROGANOFF

Veal makes a lovely, elegant substitute for the more traditional beef in this recipe, but if it's beef you're after, chuck steak or beef shin is the way to go.

SERVES: 4–6

Preparation time: 10 minutes
Cooking time: 7¼ hours (slow cooker)
2 hours (stovetop)

1 tablespoon (15 ml) olive oil
2 lb 12 oz (1.2 kg) veal blade,
    cut into 1½ inch (4 cm) pieces
3½ tablespoons (1¾ oz/50 g) butter
6 shallots, finely chopped
2 cloves garlic, finely chopped
1½ teaspoons paprika
14 ounces (400 g) mixed mushrooms,
    such as button, chestnut and portobello
2 tablespoons (30 g) tomato paste
1 cup (9 fl oz/250 ml) beef stock
1 teaspoon cornstarch – only needed for slow
    cooker
1 cup (9 fl oz/250 ml) crème fraîche or sour cream
pasta or rice, bread and parsley, to serve

IN THE SLOW COOKER

Heat the oil in a large, deep frying pan over medium–high heat. Season the veal with salt and pepper and cook for 5 minutes until browned, then transfer to the slow cooker.

Reduce the heat to medium and add the butter to the pan. Once the butter has melted, cook the shallots, garlic and paprika for 2 minutes until slightly softened. Add the mushrooms and cook for 2 minutes until slightly softened, then add the tomato paste and cook for a minute. Transfer to the slow cooker and stir in the stock. Season with salt and pepper and cook on low for 6½ hours.

In a small bowl, combine the cornstarch with a little of the cooking liquid, then stir into the stroganoff, along with the crème fraîche. Cook for 30 minutes until the veal is tender.

Serve with pasta or rice, bread and parsley.

ON THE STOVETOP

Heat the oil in a large, heavy-based saucepan over medium–high heat. Season the veal with salt and pepper and cook for 5 minutes until browned. Remove and set aside.

Reduce the heat to medium and add the butter to the pan. Once the butter has melted, cook the shallots, garlic and paprika for 2 minutes until slightly softened. Add the mushrooms and cook for 2 minutes until slightly softened, then add the tomato paste and cook for a minute. Return the meat to the pan and stir in the stock and ½ cup (4 fl oz/125 ml) of water. Season with salt and pepper. Bring to a boil, then reduce the heat to low. Cover with a lid and cook for 1½ hours until the veal is tender. Stir in the crème fraîche and cook, uncovered, for 5 minutes.

Serve with pasta or rice, bread and parsley.

RED BEANS AND RICE

This staple Creole dish was traditionally made on Mondays, using leftover pork bones from Sunday dinner, but it tastes great on any day of the week.

SERVES: 4

Preparation time: 10 minutes
Cooking time: 5½ hours (slow cooker)
2¼ hours (stovetop)

2 cups (13½ oz/380 g) red kidney beans, soaked overnight, drained and rinsed
1 smoked ham hock
1 onion, finely chopped
4 fresh or dried bay leaves
1½ tablespoons (12 g) cornstarch – only needed for slow cooker
2 stalks celery, finely chopped
1 green pepper, finely chopped
2 tablespoons (5 g) thyme leaves
3 cloves garlic, finely chopped
1 lb 2 oz (500 g) smoked pork sausage, such as andouille or chorizo, thickly sliced
1 teaspoon cayenne pepper
1 teaspoon paprika
2 cups (14 oz/400 g) long-grain rice, rinsed
finely sliced scallions, to serve

IN THE SLOW COOKER

Put the beans, ham hock, onion and bay leaves in a large saucepan and cover with 9 cups (79 fl oz/2.25 L) of cold water. Bring to a boil and cook for 30 minutes, skimming off any froth from the surface.

In a small bowl, combine ½ cup (4 fl oz/125 ml) of the cooking liquid with the cornstarch until smooth, then stir into the pan.

Transfer the mixture to the slow cooker with the celery, pepper, thyme, garlic, sausages, cayenne pepper and paprika. Season with salt and pepper, then cook on low for 4 hours.

Carefully remove the ham hock. When it is cool enough to handle, roughly shred the meat, discarding the skin and bones.

Return the meat to the slow cooker and stir well. Cook for a further hour until the ham and beans are tender. Check the seasoning.

Meanwhile, cook the rice according to the package instructions.

Serve the beans with rice and scallions.

ON THE STOVETOP

Put the beans, ham hock, onion and bay leaves in a large, heavy-based saucepan and cover with 9 cups (79 fl oz/2.25 L) of cold water. Bring to a boil, then reduce the heat and simmer for 1 hour, skimming off any froth from the surface.

Carefully remove the ham hock. When it is cool enough to handle, roughly shred the meat, discarding the skin and bones. Return the meat to the pan, then stir in the celery, pepper, thyme, garlic, sausages, cayenne pepper and paprika. Cook, uncovered, for about 1 hour, to develop the flavors and thicken the stew. Check the seasoning.

Meanwhile, cook the rice according to the package instructions.

Serve the beans with rice and scallions.

SWEET AND STICKY PORK RIBS

This is classic home-style cooking. The marinade would also work well with beef and lamb ribs, or even chicken thighs. If you're planning to make this in the slow cooker, ask the butcher to cut the ribs into shorter lengths so they'll fit.

SERVES: 4

Preparation time: 5 minutes
(+ cooling time if cooking in oven)
Cooking time: 4¼ hours (slow cooker)
2¾ hours (oven)

1 tablespoon (7 g) smoked paprika
1 teaspoon chili flakes
2 teaspoons freshly ground white pepper
3 tablespoons (45 ml) treacle or molasses
3 tablespoons (45 ml) maple syrup
1 tablespoon (18 g) sea salt flakes
4 cloves garlic, minced
1 granny smith apple, peeled, finely grated
1 tablespoon (15 ml) apple cider vinegar
4 lb 8 oz (2 kg) American-style pork ribs
green salad, to serve

IN THE SLOW COOKER

Combine the paprika, chili, pepper, treacle, maple syrup, salt, garlic, apple and vinegar in the slow cooker. Add the ribs and mix to coat well, then cook on high for 4 hours, turning the ribs halfway through.

Remove the ribs and cover loosely with foil. Pour the cooking liquid into a saucepan and bring to a boil, then reduce the heat and simmer for 15 minutes until thickened.

Brush the ribs with the sticky sauce and serve with a large green salad.

IN THE OVEN

Preheat the oven to 315°F/gas mark 2–3 (160°C) and line a roasting pan with parchment paper.

Combine the paprika, chili, pepper, treacle, maple syrup, salt, garlic, apple and vinegar in a small saucepan and bring to a boil. Reduce the heat to a simmer and cook for 10 minutes. Set the glaze aside to cool.

Add the ribs to the roasting pan and brush generously with the glaze. Cover tightly with foil and cook in the oven for 2 hours, then remove the foil and cook for another 30 minutes until tender, turning halfway through and brushing with more of the glaze.

Serve with a large green salad.

SWEDISH MEATBALLS

SERVES: 4

Preparation time: 25 minutes + 1 hour chilling
Cooking time: 4 hours (slow cooker)
1 hour 40 minutes (stovetop)

1–2 tablespoons (15–30 ml) olive oil
2 tablespoons (1 oz/30 g) butter
1 onion, finely chopped
2 slices white bread, crusts removed, roughly torn
3 tablespoons (45 ml) milk
9 ounces (250 g) ground pork
9 ounces (250 g) ground beef
1 egg, lightly beaten
¼ teaspoon ground nutmeg
¼ teaspoon ground allspice
4 tablespoons (16 g) finely chopped dill
1 tablespoon (7 g) all-purpose flour
2 cups (17 fl oz/500 ml) veal or chicken stock
3 tablespoons (45 ml) thin cream
1 tablespoon (20 g) red currant jelly
mashed potatoes, dill and red currant jelly, to serve

IN THE SLOW COOKER

Heat 1 tablespoon (15 ml) of the oil and a third of the butter in a large, heavy-based saucepan over medium heat. Cook the onion for 5 minutes until softened, then transfer to a large bowl and leave to cool completely.

Meanwhile, put the bread into a small bowl, pour over the milk and mix to combine. Set aside until the milk has been absorbed.

Add both of the ground meats, egg, nutmeg, allspice, dill and soaked bread to the bowl with the onion. Season generously with salt and pepper and mix well to combine.

Roll tablespoons of the mixture into balls and place on a lined baking sheet in a single layer. Chill in the fridge for at least 1 hour to firm.

Meanwhile, melt the remaining butter in the pan over medium heat. Add the flour and stir for 1 minute, then gradually whisk in the stock and bring to a boil. Transfer to the slow cooker, along with the meatballs.

Cook on low for 3½ hours until the meatballs are tender and cooked through.

Gently stir in the cream and red currant jelly, then cook for a further 15 minutes until warmed through.

Serve with mashed potatoes, dill sprigs and red currant jelly.

ON THE STOVETOP

Heat 1 tablespoon (15 ml) of the oil and a third of the butter in a large, heavy-based saucepan over medium heat. Cook the onion for 5 minutes until softened, then transfer to a large bowl and leave to cool completely.

Meanwhile, put the bread into a small bowl, pour over the milk and mix to combine. Set aside until the milk has been absorbed.

Add both of the ground meats, egg, nutmeg, allspice, dill and soaked bread to the bowl with the onion. Season generously with salt and pepper and mix well to combine.

Roll tablespoons of the mixture into balls and place on a lined baking sheet in a single layer. Chill in the fridge for at least 1 hour to firm.

Heat the remaining oil in the saucepan over medium–high heat. Working in batches, cook the meatballs for 5 minutes until browned all over, then remove and set aside. Melt the remaining butter in the pan. Add the flour and stir for 1 minute, then gradually whisk in the stock and bring to a boil. Reduce the heat to low, return the meatballs to the pan and cover with a lid. Cook for 1 hour, shaking the pan occasionally.

Gently stir in the cream and red currant jelly, then cook, uncovered, for 15 minutes.

Serve with mashed potatoes, dill sprigs and red currant jelly.

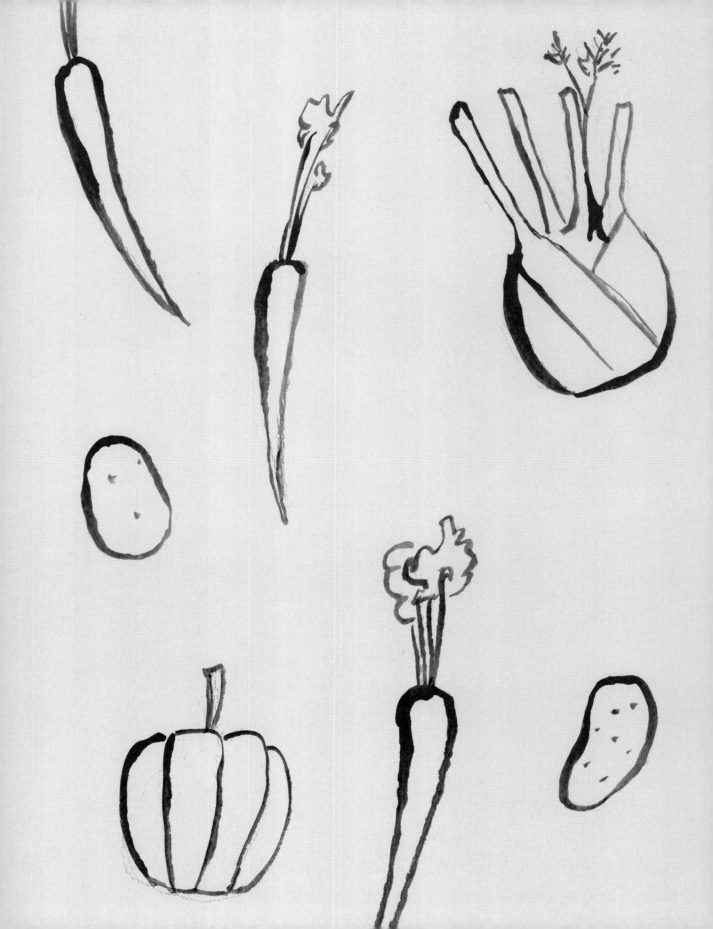

braises

GINGER AND SCALLION CHICKEN

Serve this take on Hainanese chicken with the broth poured over it or on the side. Make the chili sauce as soon as the chicken is cooking, to let the flavors mellow.

SERVES: 4

Preparation time: 15 minutes
Cooking time: 6½ hours (slow cooker)
2 hours (stovetop)

8 scallions, coarsely chopped
2½ tablespoons (20 g) finely grated ginger
10 cloves garlic, coarsely chopped
3 lb 8 oz (1.6 kg) chicken, excess fat removed
3 tablespoons (45 ml) light soy sauce
3 tablespoons (45 ml) Chinese rice wine
1 cup (9 fl oz/250 ml) chicken stock
1½ tablespoons (20 g) raw sugar
3 green or long red chilies, seeds removed, coarsely chopped
2 tablespoons (30 ml) lime juice
1 tablespoon (15 ml) sesame oil
steamed rice, kecap manis (sweet soy sauce) and sliced cucumber, to serve

SLOW COOKER

Coarsely chop the scallions, ginger and garlic in a food processor; spoon a quarter into the slow cooker and a quarter into the chicken cavity. (Keep the remaining chopped mixture for the chili sauce.) Put the chicken in the slow cooker and pour half the soy sauce and half the rice wine into the cavity.

Whisk the remaining soy sauce with the rice wine, stock, 2 teaspoons of the sugar, 1 teaspoon of salt and 11 cups (96 fl oz/2.75 L) of water in a bowl until the sugar dissolves. Pour into the slow cooker, then cook on low for 6 hours. Turn off the cooker and leave for 30 minutes.

For the chili sauce, add the chilies, lime juice and sesame oil to the mixture in the food processor, with 2 tablespoons (30 ml) water and salt to taste. Process until smooth.

Remove the chicken from the cooker. Strain the broth through a fine sieve into a saucepan and bring to a boil. Serve the chicken and broth with rice, kecap manis, sliced cucumber and the chili sauce.

ON THE STOVETOP

Coarsely chop the scallions, ginger and garlic in a food processor; spoon a quarter into a large heavy-based saucepan and a quarter into the chicken cavity. (Keep the remaining mixture for the chili sauce.) Put the chicken in the pan and pour half the soy sauce and half the rice wine into the cavity.

Whisk the remaining soy sauce with the rice wine, stock, 2 teaspoons of the sugar, 1 teaspoon of salt and 11 cups (96 fl oz/2.75 L) of water in a bowl until the sugar dissolves. Pour into the pan. Cook over very low heat for 30 minutes, then turn the chicken over, partially cover the pan with a lid and cook gently for 45 minutes (without boiling or simmering at any point). Turn the chicken over again, remove the pan from the heat, cover and set aside for 30 minutes.

For the chili sauce, add the chilies, lime juice and sesame oil to the chopped scallion mixture in the food processor, along with 2 tablespoons (30 ml) of water and salt to taste. Process until smooth.

Remove the chicken from the pan, strain the broth through a fine sieve into a clean saucepan and bring back to a boil. Serve the chicken and broth with rice, kecap manis, sliced cucumber and the chili sauce.

PORK CHEEKS BRAISED IN COCONUT WATER

In this light, nourishing Vietnamese-style braise you could easily use beef cheeks or chicken legs (with the skin removed) instead of the pork cheeks.

SERVES: 6

Preparation time: 5 minutes
Cooking time: 8 hours 20 minutes (slow cooker)
2¾ hours (stovetop)

1 tablespoon (8 g) finely grated ginger
4 red Asian shallots, thinly sliced
6 cloves garlic, finely chopped
4 cups (35 fl oz/1 L) coconut water
6 star anise
2 cinnamon sticks
8 cloves
3 tablespoons (40 g) raw sugar
3½ fl oz (100 ml) fish sauce
3 lb 5 oz (1.5 kg) skinless pork cheeks, trimmed
1 tablespoon (8 g) cornstarch –
    only needed for slow cooker
thick rice noodles, mint, Vietnamese mint and
    cilantro sprigs, roasted peanuts and sliced
    chili, to serve

IN THE SLOW COOKER

Put the ginger, shallots, garlic, coconut water, star anise, cinnamon, cloves, sugar, fish sauce and pork in the slow cooker. Cook on low for 8 hours until the pork is tender. Lift out the meat with a slotted spoon and set aside.

Turn the slow cooker up to high. In a small bowl, mix the cornstarch with ½ cup (4 fl oz/125 ml) of the braising liquid until smooth, then stir this into the slow cooker. Cook, uncovered, for 15 minutes, until slightly thickened. Meanwhile, tear the pork into large pieces and return to the slow cooker for 5 minutes to warm through.

Serve with noodles, herbs, peanuts and chili.

ON THE STOVETOP

Put the ginger, shallots, garlic, coconut water, star anise, cinnamon, cloves, sugar, fish sauce, pork and 2 cups (17 fl oz/500 ml) of water in a large, heavy-based saucepan. Bring to a boil, then reduce the heat to low. Cut out a circle of parchment paper to fit the pan and lay it directly on the surface of the liquid. Cover with a lid and cook the pork for 2 hours until tender. Lift out the meat with a slotted spoon and set aside.

Increase the heat to high and bring the braising liquid to a boil. Cook for about 30 minutes until thickened slightly, then reduce the heat to low. Tear the pork into large pieces and return to the pan for 5 minutes to warm through.

Serve with noodles, herbs, peanuts and chili.

BUFFALO CHICKEN DRUMSTICKS

These spicy chicken drumsticks are always popular, but you can use wings as per the original recipe, if you prefer. Serve with semolina (cooked in much the same way as polenta) and greens for a complete meal.

SERVES: 4

Preparation time: 5 minutes
(+ at least 4 hours marinating if cooking in oven)
Cooking time: 6 hours (slow cooker)
45 minutes (oven)

8 chicken drumsticks
8 cloves garlic, minced
3 tablespoons (45 ml) Tabasco sauce
3 tablespoons (45 ml) Mexican-style hot sauce
½ cup (4 fl oz/125 ml) chicken stock
7 tablespoons (3½ oz/100 g) butter, melted
1 tablespoon (8 g) cornstarch –
   only needed for slow cooker
semolina and spinach, to serve

IN THE SLOW COOKER

Put the chicken into the slow cooker. Whisk the remaining ingredients together in a bowl, then pour into the slow cooker. Cook on low for 6 hours until the chicken is tender.

Serve with semolina and spinach.

IN THE OVEN

In a large non-reactive bowl (or large zip-lock bag), mix together all the ingredients except the chicken. Add the chicken, then cover (or seal) and marinate in the fridge for at least 4 hours, preferably overnight.

Preheat the oven to 315°F/gas mark 2–3 (160°C). Put the chicken into a deep roasting pan, then whisk the marinade to combine and pour into the pan. Bake in the oven for about 45 minutes, turning halfway through, until the chicken is cooked through.

Serve with semolina and spinach.

NORTHERN CHINESE LAMB

Freshly toasted and ground spices make all the difference here. Serve this luscious and tender meat with plenty of rice and some steamed or stir-fried Chinese greens. If you like, you could use lamb leg in place of shoulder, or rub the same spice paste over a whole chicken or legs prior to slow cooking or roasting.

SERVES: 4

Preparation time: 10 minutes
Cooking time: 10¼ hours (slow cooker)
4¼ hours (oven)

3 teaspoons Sichuan peppercorns
3 teaspoons cumin seeds
1½ teaspoons fennel seeds
½ teaspoon ground turmeric
1 teaspoon ground ginger
2 teaspoons chili flakes
3 cloves garlic, finely chopped
1 tablespoon (15 ml) malt vinegar
3 teaspoons salt
1½ teaspoons raw sugar
4 lb 8 oz (2 kg) lamb shoulder, on the bone,
    trimmed of any excess fat
1 tablespoon (15 ml) grapeseed or rice bran oil
1 onion, cut into wedges
1 green pepper, cut into large pieces
water spinach or other Chinese greens,
    sliced green chili and rice, to serve

IN THE SLOW COOKER

Heat a heavy-based frying pan over medium heat. Toast the Sichuan peppercorns, cumin and fennel seeds for 3 minutes until fragrant, stirring so they don't burn. Use a mortar and pestle to grind coarsely, then transfer to a large bowl. Stir in the ground turmeric and ginger, together with the chili flakes, garlic, vinegar, salt and sugar.

Make 3 deep incisions in the lamb, cutting right through to the bone, then rub the spice paste all over, pushing it into the incisions.

Heat the oil in a large frying pan over high heat and sear the lamb for 5 minutes, turning until well browned on all sides.

Layer the onion and pepper in the slow cooker, then add the lamb, along with any remaining spice paste. Cook on low for 10 hours until the lamb is tender.

Serve with greens, sliced chili and rice.

IN THE OVEN

Preheat the oven to 315°F/gas mark 2–3 (160°C). Heat a heavy-based frying pan over medium heat. Toast the Sichuan peppercorns, cumin and fennel seeds for 3 minutes until fragrant, stirring so they don't burn. Use a mortar and pestle to grind coarsely, then transfer to a large bowl. Stir in the ground turmeric and ginger, together with the chili flakes, garlic, vinegar, salt and sugar.

Scatter the onion and pepper over the base of a large roasting pan. Make 3 deep incisions in the lamb, cutting right through to the bone, then rub the spice paste all over, pushing it into the incisions. Put the lamb into the tin and cover tightly with foil. Cook in the oven for 3 hours, then remove the foil and return to the oven for 1 hour or until the meat is falling off the bone, adding a little more water to the pan if needed.

Serve with greens, sliced chili and rice.

MASTER STOCK DUCK

The master stock that is left over here can be refrigerated for up to 3 days. Or store it in the freezer, where it will keep indefinitely, and use as needed. After each use, boil the stock for 10 to 15 minutes, skimming any impurities from the surface, and then strain through a fine sieve before freezing again. Looked after in this way, the flavor of your master stock will get better and better over time.

SERVES: 4

Preparation time: 5 minutes + 15 minutes resting
Cooking time: 6¼ hours (slow cooker)
1¾ hours (stovetop)

6 cups (52 fl oz/1.5 L) chicken stock
¾ cup (6 fl oz/185 ml) tamari or soy sauce
3 tablespoons (45 ml) Chinese rice wine
5½ oz (150 g) raw sugar
2 star anise
1 cinnamon stick
3 teaspoons Chinese five spice
¾ inch (2 cm) piece ginger, thinly sliced
2 cloves garlic, bruised
5 pound (2.2 kg) duck, excess fat removed
2 tablespoons (30 ml) rice bran oil or grapeseed oil
egg noodles and choy sum or other
    Chinese greens, to serve

IN THE SLOW COOKER

Combine the stock, tamari, rice wine, sugar, dried spices, ginger, garlic and 1 cup (9 fl oz/250 ml) of water in the slow cooker.

Add the duck, breast-side up. Cut out a circle of parchment paper to fit the cooker and lay it directly on the surface of the liquid. Cook on low for 6 hours until the duck is tender, turning halfway through, then remove and set aside to rest for 15 minutes.

Remove the breasts and legs from the duck. Heat the oil in a large frying pan over medium–high heat and sear the duck breasts and legs, skin-side down, for about 3 minutes until golden brown.

Meanwhile, skim any fat from the surface of the master stock, then strain the stock through a fine sieve lined with muslin or paper towel. Pour 4 cups (35 fl oz/1 L) of stock into a saucepan and bring to a boil.

Serve the duck and stock with egg noodles and Chinese greens.

ON THE STOVETOP

Combine the stock, tamari, rice wine, sugar, dried spices, ginger, garlic and 4 cups (35 fl oz/1 L) of water in a large, heavy-based saucepan. Add the duck, breast-side up, and bring to a simmer, then turn over. Cut out a circle of parchment paper to fit the pan and lay it directly on the surface of the liquid. Cover with a lid and reduce the heat to low. Cook the duck for 1 hour, turning halfway through, then remove and set aside to rest for 15 minutes.

Skim any fat from the surface of the master stock. Bring the stock to a boil, then simmer for 25 minutes. Strain through a fine sieve lined with muslin or paper towel, reserving 4 cups (35 fl oz/1 L) to serve.

Meanwhile, remove the breasts and legs from the duck carcass. Heat the oil in a large frying pan over medium–high heat and sear the duck breasts and legs, skin-side down, for about 3 minutes until golden brown.

Serve the duck and stock with egg noodles and Chinese greens.

ARGENTINIAN-STYLE LEG OF LAMB WITH CHIMICHURRI

Chimichurri is the ubiquitous bowl of sauce found on every Argentinian table. Typically served as an accompaniment to grilled meats, in this recipe it is also used as a cooking marinade. You'll need a larger slow cooker for this; if yours isn't big enough to hold a whole leg of lamb, just use the oven instead.

SERVES: 6–8

Preparation time: 15 minutes
Cooking time: 10 hours (slow cooker)
3½–4 hours (oven)

½ cup (4 fl oz/125 ml) lemon juice
½ cup (4 fl oz/125 ml) red wine vinegar
½ cup (4 fl oz/125 ml) light red wine, such as pinot noir or grenache
4 cloves garlic, coarsely chopped
1 tablespoon (3 g) dried oregano
1 teaspoon chili flakes
1 teaspoon ground cumin
1 teaspoon paprika
2 large handfuls coarsely chopped parsley
4 scallions, coarsely chopped
4 tomatoes, halved, seeds removed, coarsely grated, skins discarded
2 teaspoons salt
2 teaspoons freshly ground black pepper
½ cup (4 fl oz/125 ml) extra virgin olive oil
2 teaspoons raw sugar
3 red peppers, stems and seeds removed, coarsely chopped
5 pounds (2.2 kg) lamb leg, scored
6 fresh or dried bay leaves
green salad and crusty bread, to serve

IN THE SLOW COOKER

Put the lemon juice, vinegar, red wine, garlic, oregano, chili, cumin, paprika, parsley, scallions, tomatoes, salt and pepper in a food processor and process until finely chopped. Transfer a quarter of this to a bowl and stir in the oil, then chill until ready to serve. Stir the sugar into the remaining chimichurri.

Put the peppers into the slow cooker and place the lamb on top. Pour the chimichurri over the lamb, rubbing it all over, then add the bay leaves. Cook on low for 10 hours until tender.

Serve with the bowl of chimichurri, a green salad and crusty bread.

IN THE OVEN

Preheat the oven to 315°F/gas mark 2–3 (160°C). Put the lemon juice, vinegar, red wine, garlic, oregano, chili, cumin, paprika, parsley, scallions, tomatoes, salt and pepper in a food processor and process until finely chopped. Transfer a quarter of this to a bowl and stir in the oil, then chill until ready to serve. Stir the sugar into the remaining chimichurri.

Put the lamb into a large roasting pan and pour over the chimichurri, rubbing it all over, then add the bay leaves and 2 cups (17 fl oz/500 ml) of water. Cover tightly with foil and cook in the oven for 2 hours. Remove the foil, add the peppers and return to the oven for a further 1½ to 2 hours until tender and cooked to your liking, adding a little more water if necessary.

Serve with the bowl of chimichurri, a green salad and crusty bread.

MIDDLE EASTERN PULLED LAMB

You can use this tender, sweetly spiced lamb in myriad ways. Try it in salads, on pizzas or as a filling in phyllo pastry parcels.

SERVES: 8

Preparation time: 5 minutes
Cooking time: 8 hours (slow cooker)
3¾ hours (oven)

4 tablespoons (60 ml) pomegranate molasses
2 teaspoons ground cumin
3 teaspoons mixed spice
2 teaspoons salt
4 pounds (1.8 kg) boneless lamb shoulder, cut into large chunks
flatbread, mint, lemon wedges, pomegranate, cucumber and Greek-style yogurt, to serve

IN THE SLOW COOKER

Combine the pomegranate molasses, cumin, mixed spice, salt and ½ cup (4 fl oz/125 ml) of water in the slow cooker. Add the lamb and stir to coat. Cook on low for 8 hours until very tender. Skim any excess fat from the surface. Using two forks, pull the lamb apart. Season to taste.

Serve with warm flatbread, mint, lemon wedges, pomegranate, cucumber and Greek-style yogurt.

IN THE OVEN

Preheat the oven to 315°F/gas mark 2–3 (160°C). In a large bowl, combine the pomegranate molasses, cumin, mixed spice and salt. Add the lamb and stir to coat. Put the lamb into a large lidded casserole and pour in 14 fl oz (400 ml) of water. Cover with the lid and cook in the oven for 3 hours. Carefully remove the lid and return to the oven for a further 45 minutes until very tender. Skim any excess fat from the surface. Using two forks, pull the lamb apart. Season to taste.

Serve with warm flatbread, mint, lemon wedges, pomegranate, cucumber and Greek-style yogurt.

PORK AND PINEAPPLE TACOS

This dish originated in Central Mexico, where it is often found at street stalls. Slices of pork and chunks of pineapple are skewered and cooked on a spit over glowing coals to make something like a Mexican kebab. You should be able to find the dried chilies and small containers of chipotle chilies in adobo at specialty food shops and some supermarkets or online.

SERVES: 6

Preparation time: 15 minutes
(+ at least 2 hours marinating if cooking in oven)
Cooking time: 8 hours (slow cooker)
2½ hours (oven)

2 ancho or guajillo chilies, soaked in hot water
    until soft, stems and seeds removed
½ cup (4 fl oz/125 ml) orange juice
2 chipotle chilies in adobo sauce
3 tablespoons (45 ml) white vinegar
1 roma (plum) tomato, coarsely chopped
2 teaspoons salt
¼ teaspoon ground cloves
1 teaspoon cumin seeds
2 teaspoons dried oregano
1 onion, coarsely chopped
3 cloves garlic, coarsely chopped
1 cup (6½ oz/180 g) coarsely chopped
    sweet pineapple
3 lb 5 oz (1.5 kg) boneless pork shoulder,
    thickly sliced

Green salsa
large handful cilantro, roots scraped and
    cleaned, coarsely chopped
2 jalapeño or long green chilies, seeds removed,
    coarsely chopped
2 scallions, coarsely chopped
1 teaspoon ground cumin
1 teaspoon ground coriander
finely grated zest and juice of 1 lime
3 tablespoons (45 ml) grapeseed oil
tortillas, seared pineapple and lime wedges,
    to serve

IN THE SLOW COOKER

Place all the ingredients except the pork in a blender or food processor and process until smooth, then pour into the slow cooker. Add the pork and cook on low for 8 hours.

Meanwhile, for the green salsa, process all the ingredients in a food processor until finely chopped. Season to taste.

Serve the pork with tortillas, the green salsa, seared pineapple and lime wedges.

IN THE OVEN

Place all the ingredients except the pork in a blender or food processor and process until smooth. Pour the marinade into a large non-reactive bowl and add the pork. Mix well, then marinate in the fridge for at least 2 hours.

Preheat the oven to 315°F/gas mark 2–3 (160°C).

Transfer the pork and its marinade to a large roasting pan and cover with foil. Cook in the oven for 1½ hours, then remove the foil and return to the oven for a further hour until the pork is tender. Roughly break up the pork, return it to the pan and mix well.

Meanwhile, for the green salsa, process all the ingredients in a food processor until finely chopped. Season to taste.

Serve the pork with tortillas, the green salsa, seared pineapple and lime wedges.

SICILIAN ROAST BEEF WITH CAPONATA

Give a favorite roast a southern Italian twist with these quintessential Mediterranean flavors.

SERVES: 6

Preparation time: 10 minutes
Cooking time: 9¼ hours (slow cooker)
2½ hours (oven)

1–2 tablespoons (15–30 ml) olive oil
3 lb 2 oz (1.5 kg) beef blade roast
2 stalks celery, coarsely chopped
1 red onion, coarsely chopped
1 eggplant, coarsely chopped
1 red pepper, stems and seeds removed,
 coarsely chopped
1 can (14 ounces/400 g) chopped tomatoes
2 cloves garlic, finely chopped
3 tablespoons (30 g) capers, rinsed
3 tablespoons (30 g) coarsely chopped
 pitted kalamata olives
1 long red chili, thinly sliced
2 teaspoons raw sugar
2 tablespoons (30 ml) red wine vinegar
toasted slivered almonds and basil leaves,
 to serve

IN THE SLOW COOKER

Heat 1 tablespoon (15 ml) of oil in a large frying pan over medium–high heat. Season the beef with salt and pepper and cook for 6 minutes until browned.

Meanwhile, add the remaining ingredients to the slow cooker, season with salt and pepper, and mix to combine. Add the beef and cook on low for 9 hours until tender and cooked to your liking. Check the seasoning.

Serve with toasted slivered almonds and basil leaves.

IN THE OVEN

Preheat the oven to 315°F/gas mark 2–3 (160°C).

Heat 1 tablespoon (15 ml) of oil in a heavy-based roasting pan over medium–high heat. Season the beef with salt and pepper, then sear in the oil for 6 minutes until browned. Cover tightly with foil and roast for 1½ hours.

Meanwhile, heat another tablespoon (15 ml) of oil in a large frying pan over medium heat. Cook the celery, onion, eggplant and pepper for 5 minutes until slightly softened, then stir in the remaining ingredients. Season the caponata with salt and pepper.

Remove the foil from the pan. Add the caponata and return to the oven for a further hour until the beef is tender and cooked to your liking. Check the seasoning.

Serve with toasted slivered almonds and basil leaves.

GREEK OCTOPUS

Octopus becomes meltingly tender when cooked long and slow. Warm skordalia or white bean purée would also be beautiful with this braise.

SERVES: 4

Preparation time: 5 minutes
Cooking time: 3¼ hours (slow cooker)
2¾ hours (oven)

2 lb 4 oz (1 kg) baby octopus, cleaned
2 cups (17 fl oz/500 ml) light red wine
2 cloves garlic, finely chopped
3 tablespoons (45 ml) red wine vinegar
2 tablespoons (30 ml) extra virgin olive oil
1 tablespoon (3 g) dried oregano
1 fresh or dried bay leaf
1 cinnamon stick
2 tomatoes, halved, coarsely grated, skins discarded
pinch raw sugar
crusty bread, sliced chili, chargrilled fennel and zucchini (courgettes), lemon wedges and chopped parsley, to serve

IN THE SLOW COOKER

Put the octopus, wine and garlic into a large saucepan and bring to a boil, then let it bubble for 8 minutes to evaporate the alcohol. Transfer to the slow cooker and add the remaining ingredients. Season with salt and pepper, then cook on low for 3 hours until the octopus is tender. Check the seasoning.

Serve with crusty bread, sliced chili, chargrilled fennel and zucchini, lemon wedges and chopped parsley.

IN THE OVEN

Preheat the oven to 235°F/gas mark ½ (120°C). Put the octopus, wine and garlic into a large, flameproof casserole with a lid. Bring to a boil, then let it bubble for 8 minutes to evaporate the alcohol. Add the remaining ingredients and season with salt and pepper. Cover the casserole with the lid and cook in the oven for 2½ hours or until the octopus is tender. Check the seasoning.

Serve with crusty bread, sliced chili, chargrilled fennel and zucchini, lemon wedges and chopped parsley.

CORNED BEEF WITH ROOT VEGETABLES AND SALSA VERDE

Salsa verde adds just the right amount of freshness and zing to this comforting dish of traditional corned beef and root vegetables.

SERVES: 4

Preparation time: 10 minutes
Cooking time: 8 hours (slow cooker)
2¼ hours (stovetop)

2 lb 12 oz (1.2 kg) piece corned beef
2 fresh or dried bay leaves
4 cloves garlic, bruised
8 cloves
½ teaspoon caraway seeds
1 teaspoon black peppercorns
1 teaspoon yellow mustard seeds
8 juniper berries
8 baby pickling onions
2 turnips, cut into thin wedges
2 bunches (1 lb 10 oz/750 g) baby carrots, scrubbed, leaving ¾ inch (2 cm) greens on top

Salsa verde
handful coarsely chopped mint leaves
handful coarsely chopped basil leaves
large handful coarsely chopped parsley leaves
1 tablespoon (9 g) finely chopped capers
1 garlic clove, minced
3 tablespoons (45 ml) extra virgin olive oil
3 tablespoons (45 ml) lemon juice

IN THE SLOW COOKER

Put all the ingredients into the slow cooker with enough water to cover – about 6–8 cups (52–70 fl oz/1.5–2 L). Cook on low for 8 hours until the meat is tender.

Meanwhile, for the salsa verde, process all the ingredients in a small food processor until finely chopped. Season to taste with salt and pepper.

Serve the corned beef in chunks, along with the vegetables and dollops of salsa verde.

ON THE STOVETOP

Put the beef, bay leaves, garlic, cloves, caraway seeds, peppercorns, mustard seeds, juniper berries and onions in a large saucepan with enough water to cover – about 6–8 cups (52–70 fl oz/1.5–2 L). Bring to a boil, then reduce the heat to low, cover with a lid and simmer for 1¾ hours or until the meat is tender. Add the turnips and cook for a further 10 minutes, then add the carrots and cook for a final 5 minutes or until the vegetables are tender.

Meanwhile, for the salsa verde, process all the ingredients in a small food processor until finely chopped. Season to taste with salt and pepper.

Serve the corned beef in chunks, along with the vegetables and dollops of salsa verde.

LEMON AND CUMIN LAMB RIBS

The slow cooking of lemons with the lamb ribs adds a lovely citrus tang.
This same combination of flavors works well with lamb shoulder, helping
to cut through the richness of the meat. Cook the lamb shoulder in the same
way, then use two forks to pull it into large chunks.

SERVES: 4

Preparation time: 5 minutes
Cooking time: 8¼ hours (slow cooker)
3 hours (oven)

2 large onions, cut into wedges
8 cloves garlic, bruised
2 teaspoons extra virgin olive oil
1 tablespoon (6 g) cumin seeds, toasted
1 tablespoon (3 g) dried oregano
2 teaspoons salt
2 teaspoons freshly ground black pepper
4 lb 8 oz (2 kg) lamb ribs, trimmed, halved
2 lemons, quartered
8 sprigs lemon thyme
shaved fennel salad, to serve

IN THE SLOW COOKER

Scatter the onions and garlic in the base
of the slow cooker.

In a large bowl, combine the oil, cumin,
oregano, salt and pepper. Add the ribs
and rub to coat in the mixture.

Heat a large frying pan over medium–high
heat and cook the ribs for 3 minutes each
side until browned. Transfer to the slow
cooker, along with the lemon quarters
and thyme sprigs. Cook on low for 8 hours,
turning halfway through, until tender.

Serve the lamb with shaved fennel salad.

IN THE OVEN

Preheat the oven to 315°F/gas mark 2–3
(160°C).

Scatter the onions and garlic in a large
roasting pan.

In a large bowl, combine the oil, cumin,
oregano, salt and pepper, then add the ribs
and rub to coat in the mixture. Transfer to
the pan, along with the lemon quarters and
thyme sprigs. Cover the pan tightly with foil
and cook the lamb in the oven for 2 hours,
then remove the foil and return to the oven
for a further hour until tender.

Serve the lamb with shaved fennel salad.

curries

CAMBODIAN PEPPER PORK CURRY

If you don't have any white peppercorns, just use double the amount of black peppercorns for this beautifully balanced pork curry. For extra depth of flavor, toast the peppercorns until fragrant in a dry frying pan before grinding them.

SERVES: 4

Preparation time: 15 minutes
Cooking time: 8¼ hours (slow cooker)
1¼ hours (stovetop)

1 stem lemongrass, tough outer layers removed, white part only, finely chopped
1 teaspoon ground turmeric
1 long red chili, coarsely chopped
6 kaffir lime leaves, central ribs removed, very finely shredded
1 tablespoon (8 g) finely grated ginger
2 cloves garlic, coarsely chopped
2 teaspoons black peppercorns, coarsely ground
2 teaspoons white peppercorns, coarsely ground
2 tablespoons (30 ml) grapeseed oil or rice bran oil
9½ fl oz (270 ml) coconut cream
1 ounce (30 g) grated palm sugar or raw sugar
3 tablespoons (45 ml) fish sauce
1 lb 12 oz (800 g) pork neck, cut into 1¼ inch (3 cm) cubes
1 lb 2 oz (500 g) squash, cut into 2 inch (5 cm) wedges
brown rice, green beans, cilantro leaves and lime halves, to serve

IN THE SLOW COOKER

Put the lemongrass, turmeric, chili, lime leaves, ginger, garlic, pepper and oil in a small food processor and process to a paste.

Heat a drizzle of oil in a frying pan over medium heat and cook the curry paste for about 5 minutes until fragrant. Add the coconut cream and palm sugar and bring to a boil, then reduce to a simmer and cook for 3 minutes, without stirring, until the oil separates and rises to the surface.

Transfer to the slow cooker, then stir in the fish sauce. Add the pork and cook on low for 5 hours, then add the squash and cook for a further 3 hours until the pork and squash are tender.

Serve with steamed brown rice, green beans, cilantro leaves and lime halves.

ON THE STOVETOP

Put the lemongrass, turmeric, chili, lime leaves, ginger, garlic, pepper and oil in a small food processor and process to a paste.

Heat a drizzle of oil in a large, heavy-based saucepan over medium heat and cook the curry paste for about 5 minutes until fragrant. Add the coconut cream, palm sugar and ½ cup (4 fl oz/125 ml) of water. Bring to a boil, then reduce to a simmer and cook for 3 minutes , without stirring, until the oil separates and rises to the surface. Stir in the fish sauce. Add the pork to the pan, cover with a lid, and cook for 30 minutes until the pork is almost tender.

Stir in the squash, cover with the lid again, and cook for a further 30 minutes until the pork and squash are tender.

Serve with steamed brown rice, green beans, cilantro leaves and lime halves.

SRI LANKAN GOAT CURRY

This fiery curry is traditionally made with goat, which absorbs the flavor of spices exceptionally well. Most good butchers should be able to order some goat leg meat for you, or you could use lamb leg or shoulder meat instead, if you prefer.

SERVES: 4–6

Preparation time: 15 minutes
Cooking time: 8 hours (slow cooker)
2 hours 40 minutes (stovetop)

2 tablespoons (30 ml) coconut oil or rice bran oil
1 onion, finely chopped
4 cloves garlic, minced
2 teaspoons finely grated ginger
4 tablespoons (12 g) fresh or dried curry leaves
1 teaspoon cardamom pods, cracked
1 cinnamon stick
¼ teaspoon fenugreek seeds
1 teaspoon ground turmeric
1 teaspoon ground coriander
1 teaspon ground cumin
1 teaspoon chili powder
2 lb 4 oz (1 kg) goat leg meat,
    cut into 1 inch (2.5 cm) dice
1 can (9½ fl oz/270 ml) coconut milk
2 tomatoes, halved, coarsely grated,
    skins discarded
1 teaspoon salt
1 teaspoon raw sugar
1 stem lemongrass, bruised
1 pandan leaf, tied in a knot – optional
steamed rice, lime wedges, sliced green chili and
    coconut sambal, to serve

IN THE SLOW COOKER

Heat the oil in a heavy-based frying pan over medium heat. Cook the onion, garlic, ginger, curry leaves and all the spices for 5 minutes until the onion is translucent.

Transfer to the slow cooker, along with the remaining ingredients, and cook on low for 8 hours until the goat is tender. Check the seasoning.

Serve with steamed rice, lime wedges, sliced green chili and coconut sambal.

ON THE STOVETOP

Heat the oil in a large, heavy-based saucepan over medium heat. Cook the onion, garlic, ginger, curry leaves and all the spices for 5 minutes until the onion is translucent. Add the remaining ingredients and bring to a simmer, then reduce the heat to low and cover with a lid.

Cook for 2½ hours or until the goat is tender, stirring occasionally and adding water as necessary. Check the seasoning.

Serve with steamed rice, lime wedges, sliced green chili and coconut sambal.

YELLOW DAL WITH SPINACH

This is the simplest but most delicious dal. If you can't find chana dal, substitute yellow split peas, but keep in mind that they may take longer to cook. Serve this as part of an Indian vegetarian spread, perhaps with dal makhani (see page 127), pilaf rice and a bowl of chopped cucumber and tomato or cucumber raita. It also makes a lovely side dish with meat or fish curries and freezes particularly well.

SERVES: 4

Preparation time: 5 minutes
Cooking time: 4¼ hours (slow cooker)
45 minutes (stovetop)

3½ tablespoons (1¾ oz/50 g) butter
1 teaspoon ground turmeric
1 teaspoon chili powder
1 teaspoon cumin seeds
1 red onion, coarsely grated
1 tablespoon (8 g) finely grated ginger
2 cloves garlic, finely chopped
2 long green chilies, thinly sliced
1 cup (7 oz/200 g) chana dal, rinsed
2¾ ounces (75 g) baby spinach leaves
roti or other Indian flatbread, to serve

IN THE SLOW COOKER

Heat the butter in a frying pan over medium heat. Cook the turmeric, chili powder, cumin seeds, onion, ginger, garlic and half of the chili for about 5 minutes until fragrant and soft. Transfer to the slow cooker, then add the chana dal and 5 cups (44 fl oz/1.25 L) of water. Cook on high for 4 hours or until the dal is tender and has broken down.

Stir in the spinach and cook for 5 minutes until wilted. Season well with salt.

Serve with the remaining chili and flatbread.

ON THE STOVETOP

Heat the butter in a large, heavy-based saucepan over medium heat. Cook the turmeric, chili powder, cumin seeds, onion, ginger, garlic and half of the chili for about 5 minutes until fragrant and soft. Add the chana dal and 5 cups (44 fl oz/1.25 L) of water to the pan. Bring to a boil, then reduce the heat to low and cover with a lid. Simmer for 30 minutes, stirring occasionally, until the dal is soft and has broken down.

Stir in the spinach and cook for 3 minutes until wilted. Season well with salt.

Serve with the remaining chili and flatbread.

DAL MAKHANI

YELLOW DAL WITH SPINACH

DAL MAKHANI

This rich and robust dal from northern India is the perfect warming vegetarian meal. It also makes a lovely accompaniment to spicy grilled chicken or fish.

SERVES: 4

Preparation time: 10 minutes + overnight soaking
Cooking time: 3½ hours (slow cooker)
2 hours (stovetop)

3 tablespoons (42 g) ghee or butter
1 onion, finely chopped
2 tomatoes, coarsely chopped
2 cloves garlic, crushed
1 tablespoon (8 g) finely grated ginger
1 cinnamon stick
¾ teaspoon chili powder
1½ teaspoons ground cumin
1 tablespoon (15 g) tomato paste
⅓ cup (2½ oz/65 g) dried red kidney beans, soaked overnight, drained and rinsed
1 cup (7½ oz/210 g) black lentils, soaked overnight, drained and rinsed
4 tablespoons (60 ml) thin cream
thick yogurt, mint sprigs and roti, to serve

IN THE SLOW COOKER

Heat the ghee in a large saucepan over medium heat. Cook the onion for 4 minutes until softened. Add the tomatoes, garlic, ginger, cinnamon, chili and cumin and cook for a further 2 minutes until fragrant. Add the tomato paste and cook for 1 minute, then add the beans. Pour in 3 cups (26 fl oz/ 750 ml) of water, scraping the base of the pan to deglaze, then bring to a low boil and cook for 15 minutes.

Transfer to the slow cooker and add the lentils. Cook on high for 3 hours until the beans and lentils are tender. Discard the cinnamon stick, then season the dal with salt and stir in the cream.

Serve with yogurt, mint sprigs and roti.

ON THE STOVETOP

Heat the ghee in a large saucepan over medium heat. Cook the onion for 4 minutes until softened. Add the tomatoes, garlic, ginger, cinnamon, chili and cumin and cook for a further 2 minutes until fragrant. Add the tomato paste and cook for a further minute, then add the beans. Pour in 4 cups (35 fl oz/1 L) of water, scraping the base of the pan to deglaze. Bring to a simmer, then cover and cook for 20 minutes.

Add the lentils and cook, covered, for 1½ hours until the beans and lentils are tender. Discard the cinnamon stick, then season the dal with salt and stir in the cream.

Serve with yogurt, mint sprigs and roti.

LAMB SHANK VINDALOO

A classic hot, sour and sweet curry from Goa. The use of vinegar and garlic reflects the colonial Portuguese influence on the cuisine of this region of India.
Try this with cubed lamb, pork neck or shoulder as an alternative to lamb shanks.

SERVES: 4

Preparation time: 10 minutes
(+ 2 hours marinating if cooking in oven)
Cooking time: 8 hours (slow cooker)
2 hours 40 minutes (oven)

¾ cup (6 fl oz/185 ml) white vinegar
2–3 teaspoons chili powder
3 teaspoons ground cumin
3 teaspooons ground coriander
½ teaspoon ground cloves
¾ teaspoon ground cinnamon
1½ teaspoons ground paprika
1½ teaspoons mustard powder
3 teaspoons salt
3 teaspoons raw sugar
6 cloves garlic, minced
3 teaspoons finely grated ginger
4 x 12 ounce (350 g) lamb shanks
2 tablespoons (30 ml) rice bran or grapeseed oil
basmati rice, cucumber and mint raita
    and mint leaves, to serve

IN THE SLOW COOKER

Combine the vinegar, dried spices, salt, sugar, garlic and ginger in the slow cooker. Add the lamb shanks and rub to coat.

Heat the oil in a large frying pan over medium–high heat and brown the lamb shanks on all sides for 5 minutes, then transfer to the slow cooker. Cook on low for 8 hours until tender.

Serve with basmati rice, cucumber and mint raita and mint leaves.

IN THE OVEN

Combine the vinegar, dried spices, salt, sugar, garlic and ginger in a large, shallow dish. Add the lamb shanks and rub to coat, then marinate in the fridge for 2 hours.

Preheat the oven to 315°F/gas mark 2–3 (160°C).

Heat the oil in a large flameproof casserole over medium–high heat. Lift the lamb shanks out of the marinade, shaking off any excess, then brown in the oil for 5 minutes. Turn the heat down to low and add the marinade, together with 1 cup (9 fl oz/ 250 ml) of water. Cut out a circle of parchment paper to fit the casserole and lay it directly on the surface of the liquid. Cover with a lid, then cook in the oven for 2½ hours until tender, turning the shanks halfway through.

Serve with basmati rice, cucumber and mint raita and mint leaves.

SOUTHERN INDIAN CHICKEN CURRY

This mild coconut-based curry would also work well with skinless chicken thighs or even duck legs or breasts.

SERVES: 4

Preparation time: 5 minutes
Cooking time: 6¼ hours (slow cooker)
1 hour (stovetop)

2 tablespoons (12 g) Madras curry powder
4 chicken legs
3 tablespoons (45 ml) coconut oil or rice bran oil
1 teaspoon ground fennel
1 teaspoon brown mustard seeds
4 tablespoons (12 g) fresh or dried curry leaves
2 small onions, halved, thinly sliced
2 cloves garlic, minced
1 tablespoon (8 g) finely grated ginger
90 g (3¼ oz/1 cup) desiccated coconut
2 tomatoes, coarsely chopped
1 can (9½ fl oz/270 ml) coconut milk
crispy fried shallots, coconut cream and
    basmati rice, to serve

IN THE SLOW COOKER

Rub the curry powder and salt over the chicken to coat. Set aside until needed.

Heat half of the oil in a large frying pan over medium heat. Cook the fennel, mustard seeds, curry leaves, onions, garlic, ginger and coconut for 6 to 8 minutes until the onions are soft, stirring regularly to avoid burning the coconut. Stir in the tomatoes and coconut milk, then transfer to the slow cooker.

Heat the remaining oil in the frying pan. Add the chicken and cook for 3 minutes each side or until lightly golden. Transfer to the slow cooker, skin-side up, and mix well. Cook on low for 6 hours or until tender.

Serve the curry with crispy fried shallots, coconut cream and basmati rice.

ON THE STOVETOP

Rub the curry powder and salt over the chicken to coat. Set aside until needed.

Heat half of the oil in a large, heavy-based saucepan pan over medium heat. Cook the chicken legs for 3 minutes each side until lightly golden. Remove and set aside.

Add the remaining oil to the pan. Cook the fennel, mustard seeds, curry leaves, onions, garlic, ginger and coconut for 6 to 8 minutes until the onions are soft, stirring regularly to avoid burning the coconut.

Add the tomatoes, coconut milk and 1 cup (9 fl oz/250 ml) of water and stir well, then return the chicken to the pan, skin-side up. Bring to a simmer, then cover with a lid and reduce the heat to low. Cook for 45 minutes until the chicken is tender.

Serve the curry with crispy fried shallots, coconut cream and basmati rice.

DUCK MASSAMAN

This rich, heavily spiced Thai curry would also work well with large pieces of any red meat, such as beef chuck or shin, or lamb shoulder or leg.

SERVES: 4

Preparation time: 10 minutes
Cooking time: 4½ hours (slow cooker)
2¼ hours (stovetop)

4 duck legs
4 shallots, halved
2 cans (9½ fl oz/270 ml) coconut cream
2 cassia or cinnamon sticks
4 kaffir lime leaves
2 tablespoons (8 g) finely shredded ginger
3 medium potatoes, cut into wedges
2 tablespoons (30 g) tamarind purée
3 tablespoons (30 ml) fish sauce
1¾ ounce (50 g) grated palm sugar or raw sugar
chopped roasted peanuts, chopped cilantro and steamed rice, to serve

Curry paste
10 dried long red chilies, soaked in hot water until soft, seeds removed
½ cup (1¾ oz/45 g) dessicated coconut
4 tablespoons (35 g) unsalted roasted peanuts
6 cardamom pods, cracked, seeds removed, husks discarded
2 dried bay leaves, coarsely chopped
¼ teaspoon ground cloves

IN THE SLOW COOKER

For the curry paste, pound the ingredients to a coarse paste using a mortar and pestle.

Season the duck legs with salt and then place, skin-side down, in a large, non-stick frying pan over medium heat. Cook for 8 minutes, then turn over and cook for 2 more minutes. Transfer to the slow cooker.

Pour off all except 2 tablespoons (30 ml) of the fat from the frying pan. Add the curry paste and shallots to the pan and cook, stirring, for 3 to 5 minutes until fragrant. Add the coconut cream and cook for 6 to 8 minutes until the oil separates and rises to the surface. Stir in the remaining ingredients, then transfer to the slow cooker and cook on high for 4 hours until the potatoes and duck are tender.

Skim any fat from the surface of the curry, then serve with peanuts, cilantro and steamed rice.

ON THE STOVETOP

For the curry paste, pound the ingredients to a coarse paste using a mortar and pestle.

Season the duck legs with salt and then place, skin-side down, in a large, heavy-based saucepan over medium heat. Cook for 8 minutes, then turn over and cook for another 2 minutes. Remove and set aside.

Pour off all except 2 tablespoons (30 ml) of the fat from the pan. Add the curry paste and shallots and cook, stirring, for 3 to 5 minutes until fragrant. Add the coconut cream, cassia, lime leaves and 1 cup (9 fl oz/250 ml) of water, then cook for 6 to 8 minutes until the oil separates and rises to the surface. Return the duck to the pan, cover with a lid and cook for 1 hour, turning halfway through. Stir in the remaining ingredients, cover and cook for a further 45 minutes until the potatoes and duck are tender.

Skim any fat from the surface of the curry, then serve with peanuts, cilantro and steamed rice.

BEET CURRY

Coconut vinegar gives this exceptionally pretty and nutritious curry its distinctive flavor. You can find it at Indian supermarkets and speciality food shops, but you could use any mild white vinegar instead. Just add half the amount to start with and then adjust to taste.

SERVES: 4

Preparation time: 10 minutes
Cooking time: 7 hours (slow cooker)
1 hour 20 minutes (stovetop)

4½ tablespoons (2¼ oz/ 60 g) ghee or butter
2 small red onions, halved, thinly sliced
3 cloves garlic, finely chopped
1½ teaspoons cumin seeds
1½ teaspoons brown mustard seeds
2 tablespoons (6 g) fresh or dried curry leaves
3 long green chilies, thinly sliced
2 large bunches (3 lb 5 oz/1.5 kg) baby beets, peeled and quartered, leaves and stems kept separate and cut into 2 inch (5 cm) pieces
3½ fl oz (100 ml) coconut vinegar
1 can (14 fl oz/400 ml) coconut milk
steamed rice, to serve

IN THE SLOW COOKER

Heat the ghee in a large frying pan over medium heat and cook the onions, garlic, cumin seeds, mustard seeds, curry leaves and half the chili for 4 minutes.

Transfer to the slow cooker and add all the remaining ingredients except the beet stems and leaves. Cook on low for 6½ hours until the beets are tender. Stir in the beet stems and leaves and cook for a further 30 minutes until wilted.

Check the seasoning, then serve with the remaining chili and steamed rice.

ON THE STOVETOP

Heat the ghee in a large, heavy-based saucepan over medium heat and cook the onions, garlic, cumin seeds, mustard seeds, curry leaves and half the chili for 4 minutes. Add all the remaining ingredients except the beet stems and leaves, cover with a lid and reduce the heat to low. Cook for 1 hour until the beets are tender, stirring occasionally. Stir in the stems and leaves and cook for a further 15 minutes or until wilted.

Check the seasoning, then serve with the remaining chili and steamed rice.

SWEET JAVANESE BEEF CURRY

With its gentle flavors and mild heat, this makes a good "starter" curry for those new to curries. Even kids will be won over by its sweet, tender meat. If you can't get brisket, you could use beef shin, chuck steak or even osso buco.

SERVES: 4–6

Preparation time: 10 minutes
Cooking time: 9¼ hours (slow cooker)
2¾ hours (stovetop)

6 macadamia nuts,
   coarsely chopped
6 red Asian shallots, coarsely chopped
6 cloves garlic, coarsely chopped
1 tablespoon (8 g) finely grated ginger
½ teaspoon ground nutmeg
1 teaspoon ground white pepper
½ teaspoon ground cloves
½ teaspoon ground cinnamon
1 tablespoon (15 ml) rice bran oil or grapeseed oil
2 lb 4 oz (1 kg) beef brisket, trimmed
2 tablespoons (30 ml) white vinegar
1 stem lemongrass, bruised
4 tablespoons (60 ml) kecap manis
steamed rice, crispy fried shallots
   and boiled eggs, to serve

IN THE SLOW COOKER

For the spice paste, pound the nuts, shallots, garlic, ginger, nutmeg, pepper, cloves and cinnamon to a coarse paste using a mortar and pestle or small food processor.

Heat the oil in a large frying pan over medium heat. Season the beef with salt and cook for 5 minutes, turning, until browned, then transfer to the slow cooker.

Add the spice paste to the pan and cook for 2 to 3 minutes until fragrant, then transfer to the slow cooker. Add the remaining ingredients and 1 cup (9 fl oz/250 ml) of water. Cook on low for 9 hours until tender.

Serve with steamed rice, crispy fried shallots and boiled eggs.

ON THE STOVETOP

For the spice paste, pound the nuts, shallots, garlic, ginger, nutmeg, pepper, cloves and cinnamon to a coarse paste using a mortar and pestle or small food processor.

Heat the oil in a large, heavy-based saucepan over medium heat. Season the beef with salt and cook for 5 minutes, turning, until browned. Remove and set aside.

Add the spice paste to the pan and cook for 2 to 3 minutes until fragrant. Return the beef to the pan, then add the remaining ingredients. Pour in 3 cups (26 fl oz/750 ml) of water, or a little more if needed to partly cover the beef. Bring to a boil, then reduce the heat to low and cover with a lid. Cook for 2½ hours until the meat is tender.

Serve with steamed rice, crispy fried shallots and boiled eggs.

BEEF AND POTATO RENDANG

Full of the southeast Asian flavors of lemongrass, tamarind and coconut, this dry Indonesian curry is a real treat. If you can't find galangal, use twice as much ginger.

SERVES: 6
Preparation time: 10 minutes
Cooking time: 7 hours (slow cooker)
1 hour 35 minutes (stovetop)

3 long red chilies, roughly chopped
4 shallots, coarsely chopped
4 cloves garlic, coarsely chopped
1½ inch (4 cm) piece galangal, coarsely grated
1½ inch (4 cm) piece ginger, coarsely grated
2 teaspoons ground turmeric
2 stems lemongrass, tough outer layers removed, white parts only, bruised
2 tablespoons (10 g) desiccated coconut
1 tablespoon (13 g) raw sugar
1 tablespoon (15 g) tamarind purée
2 teaspoons ground cumin
2 teaspoons ground coriander
4 tablespoons (60 ml) grapeseed oil
2 lb 12 oz (1.2 kg) beef chuck steak, cut into 1¼ inch (3 cm) pieces
1 can (14 fl oz/400 ml) coconut milk
1 lb 5 oz (600 g) baby potatoes
steamed rice, chili and cilantro, to serve

IN THE SLOW COOKER

Put the chilies, shallots, garlic, galangal, ginger, turmeric, lemongrass, coconut, sugar, tamarind, cumin, coriander and 1 tablespoon (15 ml) of oil in a small food processor and process to a coarse paste.

Heat 2 tablespoons (30 ml) of oil in a large frying pan over medium–high heat. Season the beef with salt, add to the pan and cook for 5 minutes until browned. Add 2 tablespoons (30 ml) of water, stirring to deglaze, then transfer to the slow cooker.

Add the remaining tablespoon (15 ml) of oil to the pan and cook the spice paste, stirring, for 3 minutes until fragrant. Stir in the coconut milk and ½ cup (4 fl oz/125 ml) of water, then transfer to the slow cooker. Add the potatoes and cook on low for 7 hours until the beef and potatoes are tender.

Check the seasoning, then serve with steamed rice, chili and cilantro.

ON THE STOVETOP

Put the chilies, shallots, garlic, galangal, ginger, turmeric, lemongrass, coconut, sugar, tamarind, cumin, coriander and 1 tablespoon (15 ml) of the oil in a small food processor and process to a coarse paste.

Heat 2 tablespoons (30 ml) of oil in a large, heavy-based saucepan over medium–high heat. Season the beef with salt, add to the pan and cook for 5 minutes until browned. Add 2 tablespoons (30 ml) of water, stirring to deglaze, then remove the meat and set aside.

Add the remaining tablespoon (15 ml) of oil to the pan and cook the spice paste, stirring, for 3 minutes until fragrant, then return the beef to the pan. Stir in the coconut milk and 1 cup (9 fl oz/250 ml) of water. Bring to a simmer, then cover with a lid and reduce the heat to low. Cook for 1 hour, then add the potatoes and cook for a further 20 minutes until tender, adding more water if necessary.

Check the seasoning, then serve with steamed rice, chili and coriander.

MALAYSIAN CHICKEN CURRY

The pungent dried shrimp paste called belacan lends its elusive flavor to this curry. You should be able to find it in Asian grocers and larger supermarkets.

SERVES: 6

Preparation time: 15 minutes
Cooking time: 6½ hours (slow cooker)
1½ hours (stovetop)

¾ ounce (20 g) belacan (dried shrimp paste)
4 dried long red chilies
2 tablespoons (15 g) coriander seeds
2 teaspoons cumin seeds
½ teaspoon fennel seeds
½ teaspoon black peppercorns
1 tablespoon (6 g) finely grated fresh turmeric
    or 2 teaspoons ground turmeric
3 tablespoons (45 ml) grapeseed or rice bran oil
2 cinnamon sticks
4 cloves
6 shallots, finely chopped
4 tablespoons (15 g) curry leaves
1 can (14 fl oz/400 ml) coconut milk
½ ounce (15 g) palm sugar, coarsely grated
3 lb 5 oz (1.5 kg) chicken thighs, trimmed
4 waxy potatoes, cut into 1¼ inch (4 cm) pieces
roti and/or steamed rice, to serve

IN THE SLOW COOKER

Wrap the belacan in foil, then place in a dry frying pan together with the chilies, coriander, cumin seeds, fennel seeds and peppercorns. Toast over medium heat for 5 minutes until fragrant. Using a mortar and pestle or small food processsor, grind the dried spices to a powder, then add the belacan and turmeric to make a rough paste.

Add the oil to the frying pan and place over medium heat. Add the cinnamon, cloves, shallots and curry leaves and cook for 5 minutes until the shallots are soft. Add the spice paste and cook for 3 minutes. Stir in the coconut milk, sugar and ¾ cup (6 fl oz/185 ml) of water and cook, without stirring, for 6 to 8 minutes until the oil separates and rises to the surface.

Put the chicken and potatoes in the slow cooker, then pour in the coconut milk mixture. Cook on low for 6 hours until the chicken and potatoes are cooked through. Serve with roti and/or steamed rice.

ON THE STOVETOP

Wrap the belacan in foil, then place in a dry frying pan together with the chilies, coriander, cumin seeds, fennel seeds and peppercorns. Toast over medium heat for 5 minutes until fragrant. Using a mortar and pestle or small food processsor, grind the dried spices to a powder, then add the belacan and turmeric to make a rough paste.

Heat the oil in a large, heavy-based saucepan over medium heat. Add the cinnamon, cloves, shallots and curry leaves and cook for 5 minutes until the shallots are soft. Add the spice paste and cook for 3 minutes. Stir in the coconut milk, sugar and ¾ cup (6 fl oz/185 ml) of water. Cook, without stirring, for 6 to 8 minutes until the oil separates and rises to the surface. Add the chicken and bring to a simmer, then reduce the heat to low. Cover with a lid and cook for 30 minutes, then add the potatoes. Cook gently for another 30 minutes until the chicken and potatoes are cooked through.Serve with roti and/or steamed rice.

FISH, YOUNG COCONUT AND SWEET POTATO CURRY

You'll need a larger slow cooker for this, to hold the fish. But don't worry if yours is too small for your fish. It's just as easy to cook this delicious southeast Asian curry in the oven. Look for young coconut in Asian grocers and larger supermarkets.

SERVES: 4

Preparation time: 20 minutes
Cooking time: 2 hours (slow cooker)
1½ hours (oven)

2 tablespoons (30 ml) grapeseed or rice bran oil
4 shallots, halved, thinly sliced
4 cloves garlic, finely chopped
1 tablespoon (8 g) finely shredded ginger
3 tablespoons (18 g) curry powder
1 young coconut, juice reserved,
    flesh scooped out and thinly sliced
1 can (9½ fl oz/270 ml) coconut milk
2 tablespoons (30 ml) fish sauce
½ teaspoon raw sugar
juice of 1 lime
1 lb 2 oz (500 g) sweet potato, halved
    lengthwise, cut into ½ inch (1 cm) slices
1 lb 9 oz (700 g) snapper, cleaned
steamed brown or white rice, lime halves and
    cilantro sprigs, to serve

IN THE SLOW COOKER

Heat the oil in a frying pan over medium heat and cook the shallots, garlic, ginger and curry powder for 5 minutes. Set aside to cool.

Combine the coconut juice, flesh, milk, fish sauce, sugar and lime juice in the slow cooker, then add the sweet potato. Make two incisions in each side of the snapper, cutting right through to the bone. Rub the cooled shallot mixture all over the fish, pushing it into the incisions and cavity, then lay the fish in the slow cooker.

Cut out a circle of parchment paper to fit the cooker and lay it directly on the fish. Cook on low for 2 hours, turning halfway through, until the fish is cooked and the sweet potato is tender. Check the seasoning.

Serve with steamed rice, lime halves and cilantro sprigs.

IN THE OVEN

Preheat the oven to 275°F/gas mark 1 (140°C).

Heat the oil in a frying pan over medium heat and cook the shallots, garlic, ginger and curry powder for 5 minutes. Set aside to cool.

Combine the coconut juice, flesh, milk, fish sauce, sugar and lime juice in a baking dish long enough to hold the fish, then add the sweet potato. Make two incisions in each side of the snapper, cutting right through to the bone. Rub the cooled shallot mixture all over the fish, pushing it into the incisions and cavity, then lay the fish in the dish. Cut out a circle of parchment paper to fit the dish and lay it directly on the fish, then cover tightly with foil. Cook in the oven for 1½ hours, turning halfway through, until the fish is cooked through and the sweet potato is tender. Check the seasoning.

Serve with steamed rice, lime halves and cilantro sprigs.

JAPANESE PORK CURRY

Serve this comforting curry with noodles instead of rice, if you like. Japanese seven spice, or shichimi togarashi, is a distinctive seasoning that combines sesame seeds, chili, Sichuan pepper, dried orange peel, pepper, ginger and seaweed flakes. Available in Asian grocers and larger supermarkets, it can easily become addictive! If you can't find it, just season the curry more generously to compensate, and perhaps add some sesame seeds and a curl of orange zest if you have them on hand.

SERVES: 4

Preparation time: 10 minutes
Cooking time: 4¼ hours (slow cooker)
1¼ hours (stovetop)

3 tablespoons (1½ oz/40 g) butter
1 tablespoon (15 ml) rice bran oil
    or grapeseed oil
1 white onion, finely chopped
2 cloves garlic, finely chopped
½ cup (2¾ oz/75 g) all-purpose flour
3 tablespoons (18 g) curry powder,
    ideally Japanese or Malaysian
4 cups (35 fl oz/1 L) beef stock
½ teaspoon shichimi togarashi
2 tablespoons (30 ml) Worcestershire sauce
1 tablespoon (15 ml) tamari or soy sauce
2 teaspoons honey
1 green apple, peeled, finely grated
4 x 5½ ounces (150 g) pork neck,
    cut into large pieces
2 carrots, cut into 1¼ inch (3 cm) pieces
8 baby potatoes, peeled
snow peas, finely sliced scallions and steamed
    rice with black sesame seeds, to serve

IN THE SLOW COOKER

Heat the butter and oil in a large, deep frying pan over medium heat. Add the onion and garlic and cook for 4 minutes until softened. Stir in the flour and curry powder, then gradually pour in the stock, stirring constantly until the sauce thickens. Transfer to the slow cooker and add the remaining ingredients. Cook on low for 4 hours until the meat and vegetables are tender.

Serve with snow peas, scallions and rice.

ON THE STOVETOP

Heat the butter and oil in a large, heavy-based saucepan over medium heat. Add the onion and garlic and cook for 4 minutes until softened. Stir in the flour and curry powder, then gradually pour in the stock, stirring constantly until the sauce thickens. Add the shichimi togarashi, Worcestershire sauce, tamari, honey, apple, pork and carrots. Bring to a simmer, cover with a lid, then cook for 30 minutes until the pork is almost tender. Add the potatoes and cook, uncovered, for another 30 minutes until tender.

Serve with snow peas, scallions and rice.

BEEF AND LENTIL CURRY (HALEEM)

Traditionally, the meat in this Pakistani favorite is cooked slowly until it has completely broken down, with an almost paste-like consistency. This dish is sometimes called the "king of curries." Once you've made it, you'll know why.

SERVES: 4

Preparation time: 10 minutes
Cooking time: 5 hours (slow cooker)
2½ hours (stovetop)

1 lb 10 oz (750 g) beef shin,
  cut into 1¼ inch (3 cm) cubes
½ cup (3¼ oz/90 g) bulgur, rinsed
½ cup (3½ oz/100 g) red lentils, rinsed
½ cup (3½ oz/100 g) yellow split peas, rinsed
1 tablespoon (8 g) finely grated ginger
5 cloves garlic, minced
large pinch saffron threads
1 tablespoon (6 g) ground coriander
1 tablespoon (6 g) garam masala
2 teaspoons ground cumin
2 teaspoons ground turmeric
2 teaspoons chilli powder
3½ tablespoons (1¾ oz/50 g) ghee or butter
3 teaspoons salt
lemon halves, crispy fried shallots, cilantro
  sprigs, sliced green chili, shredded ginger and
  roti, to serve

IN THE SLOW COOKER

Put the beef, bulgur, lentils, split peas, ginger, garlic, saffron, coriander, garam masala, cumin, turmeric, chili and 3 cups (26 fl oz/750 ml) of water into the slow cooker. Cook on high for 4 hours.

Stir in the ghee and salt, then cook for a further hour until the beef has completely broken down. Check the seasoning.

Serve with lemon halves, fried shallots, cilantro, green chili, ginger and roti.

ON THE STOVETOP

Put the beef, bulgur, lentils, split peas, ginger, garlic, saffron, coriander, garam masala, cumin, turmeric, chili and 6 cups (52 fl oz/1.5 L) of water in a large, heavy-based saucepan. Bring to a boil, then reduce the heat to a simmer and cover with a lid. Cook for 2 hours until the meat has started to break down, stirring regularly.

Stir in the ghee and salt, then cook for a further 30 minutes until the beef has completely broken down, stirring regularly. Check the seasoning.

Serve with lemon halves, fried shallots, cilantro, green chili, ginger and roti.

meat-free
meals

LEEK, FENNEL AND POTATO SOUP

Cashews give this vegan soup the sort of velvety creaminess you'd usually associate with cream or butter, and the aniseed flavor of fennel marries well with the earthiness of the potatoes.

SERVES: 4–6

Preparation time: 10 minutes
Cooking time: 5 hours (slow cooker)
2¼ hours (stovetop)

3 tablespoons (45 ml) extra virgin olive oil
3 leeks, pale parts only, washed, thinly sliced
2 cloves garlic, coarsely chopped
1 fennel bulb, halved, thinly sliced
1 lb 12 oz (800 g) potatoes,
   cut into 1½ inch (4 cm) pieces
6 cups (52 fl oz/1.5 L) vegetable stock
4 tablespoons (30 g) raw cashews
2 teaspoons fennel seeds, toasted,
   coarsely ground
ground fennel, chopped chives and crusty bread,
   to serve

IN THE SLOW COOKER

Put all the ingredients into the slow cooker and season with salt and pepper. Cook on high for 5 hours until all the vegetables are tender.

Using a blender or immersion blender, purée the soup in batches until smooth, then check the seasoning.

Serve with ground fennel, chopped chives and crusty bread.

ON THE STOVETOP

Heat the oil in a large, heavy-based saucepan over medium heat and cook the leeks, garlic and fennel for 6 to 8 minutes until softened. Add the remaining ingredients and season well with salt and pepper. Bring to a boil, then reduce the heat to low, cover with a lid and cook for 2 hours until all the vegetables are tender.

Using a blender or stick blender, purée the soup in batches until smooth, then check the seasoning.

Serve with ground fennel, chopped chives and crusty bread.

SOUTH AFRICAN RED KIDNEY BEAN CURRY

South African cuisine celebrates a medley of flavors, as this robust kidney bean curry demonstrates. Serve over a bowl of steamed rice for a simple but satisfying meal.

SERVES 4

Preparation time: 15 minutes + overnight soaking
Cooking time: 3½ hours (slow cooker)
2½ hours (stovetop)

2 tablespoons (28 g) ghee or butter
1 large brown onion, coarsely chopped
3 cloves garlic, finely chopped
3 small green chilies, finely chopped
1 tablespoon (8 g) finely grated ginger
½ teaspoon brown mustard seeds
½ teaspoon asafoetida
½ teaspoon ground coriander
2 teaspoons garam masala
1 dried long red chili
3 tomatoes, finely chopped
3 tablespoons (6 g) curry leaves
2 teaspoons tomato paste
1½ cups (10¼ oz/290 g) dried red kidney beans,
   soaked overnight, drained and rinsed
flatbread, fried curry leaves and chopped
   tomato and cucumber, to serve

IN THE SLOW COOKER

Heat the ghee in a saucepan over medium heat and cook the onion for 4 minutes until softened. Add the garlic, green chilies, ginger and dried spices and cook for 2 minutes until fragrant. Transfer to the slow cooker, along with the tomatoes, curry leaves and tomato paste.

Add the beans to the saucepan, then pour in 2 cups (17 fl oz/500 ml) of water. Bring to a boil and cook for 15 minutes, then transfer to the slow cooker. Cook on high for 3 hours.

Season to taste with salt and pepper, then serve with flatbread, fried curry leaves and chopped tomato and cucumber.

ON THE STOVETOP

Heat the ghee in a large, heavy-based saucepan over medium heat and cook the onion for 4 minutes until softened. Add the garlic, green chilies, ginger and dried spices and cook for 2 minutes until fragrant.

Add the tomatoes, curry leaves, tomato paste and beans to the pan. Pour in 2½ cups (21½ fl oz/625 ml) of water and bring to a boil. Reduce the heat to a simmer and cook for 2 to 2½ hours until the beans are tender, adding more water if needed.

Season to taste with salt and pepper, then serve with flatbread, fried curry leaves and chopped tomato and cucumber.

CHUNKY TOMATO SOUP

There's nothing like a fresh tomato soup, and this basil-infused one is delicious. For a more susbtantial version, try it with the cheesy agnolotti on page 53.

SERVES: 4–6

Preparation time: 20 minutes
Cooking time: 3¼ hours (slow cooker)
1¼ hours (stovetop)

3 lb 5 oz (1.5 kg) mixed large tomatoes
4 tablespoons (60 ml) extra virgin olive oil,
    plus extra for drizzling
2 shallots, roughly chopped
4 cloves garlic, finely chopped
large handful basil sprigs, tied together
    with string
4 cups (35 fl oz/1 L) vegetable stock
2 teaspoons salt
2 teaspons freshly ground black pepper
1–2 teaspoons raw sugar, to taste
basil leaves and crusty bread, to serve

IN THE SLOW COOKER

Score a cross in the base of the tomatoes, then put into a heatproof bowl. Cover with boiling water and leave for 1 minute until the skins start to come away from the flesh. Drain, then peel. Remove the cores from the tomatoes and coarsely chop the flesh.

Heat the oil in a frying pan over low heat and cook the shallots and garlic for 5 minutes until translucent, then transfer to the slow cooker. Add the remaining ingredients and cook on low for 3 hours.

Transfer half the soup to a heatproof bowl. Purée with an immersion blender until smooth, then return to the slow cooker and cook for 5 minutes to warm through. Check the seasoning, then drizzle with a little olive oil.

Serve with basil leaves and crusty bread.

ON THE STOVETOP

Score a cross in the base of the tomatoes, then put into a heatproof bowl. Cover with boiling water and leave for 1 minute until the skins start to come away from the flesh. Drain, then peel. Remove the cores from the tomatoes and coarsely chop the flesh.

Heat the oil in a large, heavy-based saucepan over low heat and cook the shallots and garlic for 5 minutes until translucent. Add the remaining ingredients, increase the heat to medium and bring to a boil. Reduce the heat to low, cover with a lid and simmer for 1 hour.

Transfer half the soup to a heatproof bowl. Purée with an immersion blender until smooth, then return to the pan and heat for 5 minutes to warm through. Check the seasoning, then drizzle with a little olive oil.

Serve with basil leaves and crusty bread.

BORSCHT

A strikingly colored, velvety soup that tastes every bit as good as it looks. Serve this the Russian way with rye croutons, sour cream and dill.

SERVES: 4–6

Preparation time: 10 minutes
Cooking time: 7 hours (slow cooker)
1½ hours (stovetop)

2 lb 4 oz (1 kg) beets,
  cut into 1¼ inch (3 cm) pieces
1 onion, finely chopped
6 cups (52 fl oz/1.5 L) vegetable stock
14 ounces (400 g) potatoes
3 tablespoons (9 g) finely chopped dill stems
1 fresh or dried bay leaf
rye croutons, dill sprigs and sour cream
  or crème fraîche, to serve

IN THE SLOW COOKER

Put the beets, onion, stock, potatoes, dill stems and bay leaf into the slow cooker. Season with salt and pepper, then cook on high for 7 hours until the beets are tender.

Remove the bay leaf and discard. Using a blender or immersion blender, purée the soup in batches until smooth. Check the seasoning.

Serve with rye croutons, dill sprigs and sour cream or crème fraîche.

ON THE STOVETOP

Put the beets, onion, stock, potatoes, dill stems and bay leaf into a large, heavy-based saucepan. Season with salt and pepper, then bring to a boil. Reduce the heat to a simmer, cover with a lid and cook for 1½ hours until the beets are tender.

Remove the bay leaf and discard. Using a blender or immersion blender, purée the soup in batches until smooth. Check the seasoning.

Serve with rye croutons, dill sprigs and sour cream or crème fraîche.

MOROCCAN FAVA BEAN SOUP

With this beautifully thick and creamy bean soup, vegans need not miss out on the simple pleasure of a comforting bowl of soup on a cold winter's night.

SERVES: 6

Preparation time: 20 minutes + overnight soaking
Cooking time: 3¼ hours (slow cooker)
1½ hours (stovetop)

3 cups (1 lb 4½ oz/570 g) large fava beans (dried broad beans), soaked overnight, drained and rinsed
2 tablespoons (30 ml) olive oil
1 large brown onion, chopped
4 cloves garlic, finely chopped
1 teaspoon ground cumin
1 teaspoon ground coriander
½ teaspoon sweet paprika
2 cups (17 fl oz/500 ml) vegetable stock
1 large potato, peeled, cut into large pieces
finely grated zest and juice of 1 lemon
chopped cilantro, paprika and extra virgin olive oil, to serve

IN THE SLOW COOKER

Remove the skins from the fava beans.

Heat the oil in a large saucepan over medium heat. Add the onion, garlic and spices and cook for 3 to 5 minutes until the onion has softened slightly. Add the beans and 4 cups (35 fl oz/1 L) of water and bring to a boil. Cook for 10 minutes, then transfer to the slow cooker, along with the stock and potato. Cook on high for 3 hours until the beans and potato are tender.

Using a blender or immersion blender, purée the soup in batches until smooth, adding the lemon juice and zest, plus a little water if the soup is too thick.

Season to taste, then serve with cilantro, paprika and extra virgin olive oil.

ON THE STOVETOP

Remove the skins from the fava beans.

Heat the oil in a large saucepan over medium heat. Add the onion, garlic and spices and cook for 3 to 5 minutes until the onion has softened slightly. Add the beans, potato, stock and 6 cups (52 fl oz/1.5 L) of water. Bring to a boil, then reduce to a simmer, cover with a lid and cook for 1¼ hours until the beans and potato are tender.

Using a blender or immersion blender, purée the soup in batches until smooth, adding the lemon juice and zest, plus a little water if the soup is too thick.

Season to taste, then serve with cilantro, paprika and extra virgin olive oil.

TAMARIND AND PUMPKIN SAMBAR

Serve this light, hot and sour South Indian lentil and vegetable stew with roti or rice.

SERVES: 4
Preparation time: 15 minutes + 30 minutes soaking
Cooking time: 4 hours (slow cooker)
35 minutes (stovetop)

1½ cups (10½ oz/300 g) yellow lentils, soaked
   for 30 minutes, drained and rinsed
2 lb 4 oz (1 kg) sugar pumpkin,
   cut into ¾ inch (2 cm) slices
2 tablespoons (28 g) ghee or butter
1 onion, finely chopped
2 cloves garlic, finely chopped
2 teaspoons brown mustard seeds
2 tablespoons (6 g) curry leaves
1 tablespoon (15 g) tamarind concentrate
cilantro sprigs, to serve

Sambar spice mix
1 teaspoon coriander seeds
1 teaspoon cumin seeds
½ teaspoon fenugreek seeds
½ teaspoon black peppercorns
1 teaspoon chili flakes
1 tablespoon (5 g) desiccated coconut
1 teaspoopn ground turmeric
½ teaspoon ground cinnamon

IN THE SLOW COOKER

Put the lentils in the slow cooker with
3 cups (26 fl oz/750 ml) of water. Cook
on high for 2 hours. Add the pumpkin and
cook for another hour.

For the sambar spice mix, toast the
coriander, cumin and fenugreek seeds,
peppercorns, chili and coconut in a dry
frying pan until fragrant, stirring so they
don't burn. Grind to a fine powder using
a small food processor or spice grinder,
then transfer to a bowl and stir in the
turmeric and cinnamon.

Heat the ghee in a frying pan over medium
heat and cook the onion, garlic, mustard
seeds and curry leaves for about 5 minutes
until the onion is soft. Stir in the sambar
powder, tamarind and 1 cup (9 fl oz/250 ml)
of water, then transfer to the slow cooker.
Turn the pumpkin and cook for a further
1 to 1½ hours until the lentils and pumpkin
are tender. Season with salt, then top with
cilantro sprigs.

ON THE STOVETOP

Put the lentils and pumpkin in a large
saucepan with 4 cups (35 fl oz/1 L) of water
and bring to a boil. Reduce the heat to a
simmer and cook for 20 minutes until just
tender, skimming off any impurities.

For the sambar spice mix, toast the
coriander, cumin and fenugreek seeds,
peppercorns, chili and coconut in a dry
frying pan until fragrant, stirring so they
don't burn. Grind to a fine powder using
a small food processor or spice grinder,
then transfer to a bowl and stir in the
turmeric and cinnamon.

Heat the ghee in a large frying pan over
medium heat and cook the onion, garlic,
mustard seeds and curry leaves for about
5 minutes until the onion is soft. Add the
spice paste and cook for 3 minutes, stirring,
until fragrant. Stir in the tamarind and
1 cup (9 fl oz/250 ml) of water and bring to
a boil, then tip into the pan with the lentils
and pumpkin. Cook for a further 5 minutes
until the lentils and pumpkin are tender.
Season with salt, then top with cilantro sprigs.

CAULIFLOWER, CELERIAC AND SQUASH LASAGNA

SERVES: 6

Preparation time: 30 minutes
Cooking time: 4¼ hours (slow cooker)
1¼ hours (oven)

½ small cauliflower, coarsely chopped
1 lb 2 oz (500 g) celeriac, peeled, thinly sliced
21 fl oz (600 ml) milk
5½ ounces (150 g) blue cheese, crumbled
2 tablespoons (5 g) finely chopped sage
1¾ cups (6½ oz/180 g) finely grated parmesan
2 lb 4 oz (1 kg) butternut squash, peeled, cut
   into ¼ inch (5 mm) slices
3 zucchini, cut lengthwise into ¼ inch (5 mm)
   slices
4½ ounces (125 g) instant lasagna sheets
green salad, to serve

IN THE SLOW COOKER

Process the cauliflower in a food processor until finely chopped, then set aside.

Put the celeriac, milk and 1 cup (9 fl oz/ 250 ml) of water in a saucepan over medium heat. Cut out a circle of parchment paper to fit the pan and lay it directly on the surface of the liquid. Bring to a simmer and cook the celeriac for 12 minutes until very tender. Strain, reserving both the celeriac and its cooking liquid. Put the celeriac and 1 cup (9 fl oz/250 ml) of its cooking liquid into the food processor with the blue cheese, sage and about half the parmesan. Purée until smooth, then season with salt and pepper.

Grease the slow cooker with oil. Spread 4 tablespoons (60 ml) of the celeriac sauce over the base, followed by quarter of the cauliflower, a layer of pumpkin and a layer of zucchini. Spread over another 4 tablespoons (60 ml) of the sauce, then a layer of lasagna sheets. Repeat these layers until all the ingredients are used up, finishing with sauce and cauliflower. Scatter over the remaining parmesan and cook on low for 4 hours until cooked through.

Serve with a green salad.

IN THE OVEN

Preheat the oven to 350°F/gas mark 4 (180°C) and oil an 8 cup (70 fl oz/2 L) baking dish.

Process the cauliflower in a food processor until finely chopped, then set aside.

Put the celeriac, milk and 1 cup (9 fl oz/ 250 ml) of water in a saucepan over medium heat. Cut out a circle of parchment paper to fit the pan and lay it directly on the surface of the liquid. Bring to a simmer and cook the celeriac for 12 minutes until very tender. Strain, reserving both the celeriac and its cooking liquid. Put the celeriac and 1 cup (9 fl oz/250 ml) of its cooking liquid into the food processor with the blue cheese, sage and about half the parmesan. Purée until smooth, then season with salt and pepper.

Spread 4 tablespoons (60 ml) of the celeriac sauce over the base of the dish, followed by quarter of the cauliflower, a layer of pumpkin and a layer of zucchini. Spread over another 4 tablespoons (60 ml) of the sauce, then a layer of lasagna sheets. Repeat these layers until all the ingredients are used up, finishing with sauce and cauliflower. Scatter over the remaining parmesan, cover with foil and bake for 30 minutes. Remove the foil and return to the oven for another 30 minutes until golden and cooked through.

Serve with a green salad.

SICHUAN CHILI EGGPLANT AND SOYBEANS

Feel free to adjust the amount of chili, depending on your heat tolerance. Cubes of firm tofu or green beans can be used in place of the soybeans.

SERVES: 4

Preparation time: 10 minutes + 1 hour standing
Cooking time: 2¾ hours (slow cooker)
1 hour (stovetop)

2 lb 12 oz (1.25 kg) eggplants, quartered lengthwise then cut into 1¼ inch (3 cm) slices
1½ tablespoons (22 ml) sesame oil
4 cloves garlic, finely chopped
2 teaspoons Sichuan peppercorns, toasted, coarsely crushed
2 teaspoons finely grated ginger
4 tablespoons (60 ml) Chinese rice wine
4 tablespoons (60 ml) oyster sauce
1 teaspoon chili flakes
3 tablespoons (45 ml) light soy sauce
1½ tablespoons (22 ml) malt vinegar
1 tablespoon (13 g) coconut sugar or raw sugar
1 tablespoon (8 g) cornstarch
4 scallions, thinly sliced, white and pale parts kept separate from green parts
1½ cups (7¾ oz/220 g) frozen shelled soybeans (edamame), thawed
roasted peanuts, sliced red chili, chopped cilantro and steamed rice, to serve

IN THE SLOW COOKER

Sprinkle the eggplant with salt and set aside in a large colander set over a bowl for 1 hour.

Rinse the eggplant and pat dry with paper towel. Working in batches, heat 2 teaspoons of the oil in a large frying pan or wok over medium–high heat and sear a third of the eggplant for 2 minutes each side, then transfer to the slow cooker. Repeat with the remaining oil and eggplant.

In a bowl, combine the garlic, peppercorns, ginger, rice wine, oyster sauce, chili flakes, soy sauce, vinegar, sugar, cornstarch, the white and pale green parts of the scallion and 1 cup (9 fl oz/250 ml) of water. Whisk well, then transfer to the slow cooker. Cook on high for 2¼ hours, then stir in the soybeans and cook for a further 15 minutes.

Scatter with the scallion greens, peanuts, chili and cilantro, then serve with rice.

ON THE STOVETOP

Sprinkle the eggplant with salt and set aside in a large colander set over a bowl for 1 hour.

Rinse the eggplant and pat dry with paper towel. Working in batches, heat 2 teaspoons of the oil in a large heavy-based saucepan over medium–high heat and sear a third of the eggplant for 2 minutes each side, then transfer to the slow cooker. Repeat with the remaining oil and eggplant, then return all the eggplant to the pan.

In a bowl, combine the garlic, peppercorns, ginger, rice wine, oyster sauce, chili flakes, soy sauce, vinegar, sugar, cornstarch, the white and pale green parts of the scallions and 1 cup (9 fl oz/250 ml) of water. Whisk well, then add to the saucepan. Cover with a lid and simmer for 45 minutes until the eggplant is tender. Stir in the soybeans and cook for 5 minutes to warm through.

Scatter with the scallion greens, peanuts, chili and cilantro, then serve with rice.

CHERMOULA ROOT VEGETABLE TAGINE

Often used with meat and fish, North African chermoula paste adds zesty notes to simply cooked root vegetables in this tagine. Serve with quinoa or couscous for a light but warming supper.

SERVES: 4

Preparation time: 10 minutes
Cooking time: 3 hours (slow cooker)
50 minutes (stovetop)

1 small celeriac, peeled, cut into
   1½ inch (4 cm) chunks
1 bunch radishes, any larger ones halved
1 bunch baby beets, peeled,
   any larger ones halved
1 bunch baby carrots, scrubbed,
   leaving ¾ inch (2 cm) greens on top

Chermoula
3 tablespoons (45 ml) extra virgin olive oil
2 cloves garlic, finely chopped
2 teaspoons finely grated ginger
1 large red onion, coarsely grated
½ teaspoon chili flakes
½ teaspoon ground turmeric
1½ teaspoons ground cumin
4 tablespoons (16 g) finely chopped parsley
4 tablespoons (4 g) finely chopped cilantro
3 tablespoons finely chopped preserved
   lemon rind
pinch saffron threads, soaked in 1 tablespoon
   (15 ml) hot water

IN THE SLOW COOKER

For the chermoula, place all the ingredients and 4 tablespoons (60 ml) of water in the slow cooker. Mix well to combine, then season with salt and pepper.

Add the celeriac, radishes and beets to the slow cooker and toss to coat. Cook on high for 1 hour, then add the carrots and cook for a further 2 hours until the vegetables are tender. Check the seasoning.

ON THE STOVETOP

For the chermoula, heat the oil in a large, heavy-based saucepan over medium heat. Add the garlic, ginger, onion, chili, turmeric and cumin and cook for 5 minutes until the onion has softened. Stir in the parsley, cilantro, preserved lemon rind and the saffron with its soaking liquid.

Add all the vegetables and 1 cup (9 fl oz/250 ml) of water to the pan. Stir to coat in the chermoula, then reduce the heat to low, cover with a lid and cook for 40 minutes until the vegetables are tender. Check the seasoning.

BLACK BEAN AND SPINACH ENCHILADAS

SERVES: 4

Preparation time: 25 minutes + overnight soaking
Cooking time: 2 hours 40 minutes (slow cooker)
1 hour (oven)

1 cup (7¾ oz/220 g) black beans, soaked overnight
1 tablespoon (15 ml) grapeseed oil or rice bran oil
1 onion, finely chopped
2 cloves garlic, finely chopped
1 bunch spinach, washed, coarsely chopped
2 cans (14 oz/400 g) chopped tomatoes
2 teaspoons ground cumin
1 tablespoon (7 g) smoked paprika
2 long green chilies, finely chopped
handful coriander (cilantro) roots and stems,
    cleaned, finely chopped
1 teaspoon raw sugar
2 teaspoons lime juice
1½ cups (5½ oz/150 g) grated cheddar cheese
12 corn or small flour tortillas

Chunky guacamole
2 ripe avocados, halved
3½ ounces (100 g) cherry tomatoes
handful cilantro leaves, chopped
finely grated zest and juice of 1 lime
1 long green chili, finely chopped

IN THE SLOW COOKER

Put the beans into a large saucepan and cover with water. Bring to a boil, then simmer for 30 minutes until almost tender. Drain and rinse, then set aside in a bowl.

Meanwhile, heat the oil in a large frying pan over medium heat. Cook the onion and garlic for 5 minutes until the onion is soft. Add the spinach and cook for 2 minutes until wilted. Season and add to the bowl of beans.

Add the tomatoes, cumin, paprika, chilies, cilantro roots and stems, sugar and lime juice to the pan. Cook for 2 minutes, stirring, then season. Stir 1 cup (9 fl oz/250 ml) of this tomato sauce and a third of the cheese into the bean mixture, then spoon 4 tablespoons onto each tortilla and roll up to enclose.

Evenly spread ½ cup (4 fl oz/125 ml) of the sauce over the base of the slow cooker. Lay the enchiladas on top, seam-side down, covering each layer with sauce and cheese. Cook on low for 2 hours.

For the guacamole, mash the avocados and tomatoes with a fork. Stir in the remaining ingredients and season to taste.

Serve the enchiladas with the guacamole.

IN THE OVEN

Put the beans into a large saucepan and cover with water. Bring to a boil, then simmer for 30 minutes until almost tender. Drain and rinse, then set aside in a bowl.

Meanwhile, preheat the oven to 350°F/gas mark 4 (180°C). Heat the oil in a large frying pan over medium heat. Cook the onion and garlic for 5 minutes until the onion is soft. Add the spinach and cook for 2 minutes until wilted. Season and add to the bowl of beans.

Add the tomatoes, cumin, paprika, chilies, cilantro roots and stems, sugar and lime juice to the pan. Cook for 2 minutes, stirring, then season. Stir 1 cup (9 fl oz/250 ml) of this tomato sauce and a third of the cheese into the bean mixture, then spoon 4 tablespoons onto each tortilla and roll up to enclose.

Evenly spread 1 cup (9 fl oz/250 ml) of the sauce in a large roasting pan. Place the enchiladas on top, seam-side down, then spoon over the rest of the sauce and cheese. Bake for 25 minutes until golden.

For the guacamole, mash the avocados and tomatoes with a fork. Stir in the remaining ingredients and season.

Serve the enchiladas with the guacamole.

LENTILS WITH CHARD, DILL AND FETA

Serve this as a side dish or a fresh and filling lunch. Remember the feta will be salty, so go easy on the salt when seasoning.

SERVES: 4

Preparation time: 5 minutes
Cooking time: 3¼ hours (slow cooker)
35 minutes (stovetop)

2 cups (14 oz/400 g) puy-style lentils, rinsed
4 cups (35 fl oz/1 L) vegetable stock
2 cloves garlic, finely chopped
1 lb 10 oz (750 g) rainbow chard, leaves finely
    shredded, stems cut into ¾ inch (2 cm) dice
handful coarsely chopped dill
2 scallions, thinly sliced
7 ounces (200 g) feta, broken into pieces
extra virgin olive oil and lemon wedges, to serve

IN THE SLOW COOKER

Put the lentils, stock and garlic into the slow cooker and cook on high for 3 hours until the lentils are tender. Stir in the chard and cook for a further 15 minutes until wilted. Season with salt and pepper, then stir in half of each of the dill, scallions and feta.

Top with the remaining dill, scallions and feta. Serve with olive oil and lemon wedges.

ON THE STOVETOP

Put the lentils, stock and garlic in a large, heavy-based saucepan and bring to a boil, then reduce the heat to simmer. Cook for about 15 minutes until the lentils are almost tender. Stir in the chard, cover with a lid and cook for a further 10 minutes until wilted. Season with salt and pepper, then stir in half of each of the dill, scallions and feta.

Top with the remaining dill, scallions and feta. Serve with olive oil and lemon wedges.

BOSTON BEANS

This is a twist on the classic Boston baked beans, which are usually made with pork. Smoked paprika adds similar depth of flavor without the meat. This makes a great breakfast on brisk mornings.

SERVES: 4

Preparation time: 5 minutes + overnight soaking
Cooking time: 8¼ hours (slow cooker)
3¼ hours (stovetop)

13 ounces (375 g) great northern, navy or haricot beans, soaked overnight, drained and rinsed
1 onion, finely chopped
2 cups (17 fl oz/500 ml) vegetable stock
2 tablespoons (30 ml) maple syrup
2 tablespoons (30 ml) treacle or molasses
1 tablespoon (7 g) smoked paprika
½ teaspoon cayenne pepper
2 cloves garlic, finely chopped
2 tablespoons (30 ml) dijon mustard
1 can (14 ounces/400 g) chopped tomatoes
1 fresh or dried bay leaf
toasted crusty bread and parsley leaves, to serve

IN THE SLOW COOKER

Put the beans, onion, stock and 2 cups (17 fl oz/500 ml) of water in a saucepan and bring to a boil. Cook for 10 minutes, skimming any impurities from the surface.

Transfer the contents of the saucepan to the slow cooker. Add the remaining ingredients and cook on low for 8 hours until the beans are tender.

Serve with toasted crusty bread and parsley.

ON THE STOVETOP

Put all the ingredients into a large, heavy-based saucepan. Pour in 2 cups (17 fl oz/500 ml) of water and bring to a boil, then reduce the heat to a simmer and cover with a lid. Cook for 3 hours until the beans are tender, stirring occasionally. Remove the lid for the last hour of cooking and add some more water if needed.

Serve with toasted crusty bread and parsley.

PARSNIPS AND CARROTS WITH BLACK BEAN SAUCE

You should be able to find fermented black beans at Asian grocers and larger supermarkets. Their pungent saltiness brings these root vegetables to life.

SERVES: 4

Preparation time: 5 minutes
Cooking time: 2 hours (slow cooker)
35 minutes (stovetop)

1 tablespoon (15 ml) sesame oil
4 tablespoons (60 ml) Chinese rice wine
2 tablespoons fermented black beans,
    rinsed and coarsely chopped
2 tablespoons (15 g) finely grated ginger
1½ teaspoons black peppercorns,
    coarsely ground
2 cloves garlic, minced
1 teaspoon raw sugar
1 tablespoon (15 ml) tamari or light soy sauce
1 tablespoon (15 ml) malt vinegar
3 parsnips, quartered and tough cores removed
4 carrots, cut into chunks
sliced scallion and steamed rice, to serve

IN THE SLOW COOKER

Combine the sesame oil, rice wine, black beans, ginger, pepper, garlic, sugar, tamari, vinegar and 3 tablespoons (45 ml) of water in the slow cooker. Add the parsnips and carrots and mix to coat. Cook on high for 2 hours until tender.

Serve with scallion and steamed rice.

ON THE STOVETOP

Heat the oil in a wok or large frying pan over medium–high heat. Cook the parsnips and carrots for 10 minutes until lightly golden, then reduce the heat to low.

Add the remaining ingredients, along with ½ cup (4 fl oz/125 ml) of water. Cook for 25 minutes, stirring regularly, until the parsnips and carrots are tender.

Serve with scallion and steamed rice.

QUINOA, KALE AND RICOTTA CAKE

You can mix it up and use spinach with the kale. We used a 22 cup (192 fl oz/5.5 L) slow cooker for this recipe. Remember that cooking times may vary depending on the capacity of your cooker, so if yours is bigger or smaller than this, keep an eye on things for the last hour or so of cooking.

SERVES: 6

Preparation time: 10 minutes
Cooking time: 4¼ hours (slow cooker)
1½ hours (oven)

1 cup (7 oz/200 g) tri-color (red, black
  and white) quinoa or red quinoa, rinsed
4 cups (10½ oz/300 g) finely shredded
  kale leaves
2 tablespoons (30 ml) extra virgin olive oil
2 scallions, thinly sliced
4 cloves garlic, finely chopped
1 lb 5 oz (600 g) ricotta
4 eggs, lightly beaten
1 cup (2¾ oz/80 g) finely grated parmesan
large handful coarsely chopped parsley
handful coarsely chopped mint
cucumber chunks and mint sprigs, dressed
  with olive oil and lemon juice, to serve

IN THE SLOW COOKER

Grease the slow cooker with oil and line with parchment paper.

Put the quinoa into a saucepan and cover with 4 cups (35 fl oz/1 L) of water. Bring to a boil, then cover with a lid and reduce the heat to low. Cook for 10 minutes, then add the kale and cook for another 2 minutes. Drain the quinoa and kale, then refresh under cold running water.

Combine the remaining ingredients in a large bowl and season well with salt and pepper. Add the quinoa and kale and mix thoroughly, then spoon into the slow cooker, smoothing the surface of the cake.

Cover the lid of the slow cooker with a clean tea towel, securing the corners around the knob with string or an elastic band – this is to prevent any condensation from dripping onto the cake. Cook on low for 4 hours until set and cooked through.

Serve with cucumber and mint salad.

IN THE OVEN

Preheat the oven to 350°F/gas mark 4 (180°C). Grease and line a 8½ inch (22 cm) springform cake pan.

Put the quinoa into a saucepan and cover with 4 cups (35 fl oz/1 L) of water. Bring to a boil, then cover with a lid and reduce the heat to low. Cook for 10 minutes, then add the kale and cook for another 2 minutes. Drain the quinoa and kale, then refresh under cold running water.

Combine the remaining ingredients in a large bowl and season well with salt and pepper. Add the quinoa and kale and mix thoroughly, then spoon into the pan, smoothing the surface of the cake.

Cook in the oven for 1¼ hours until set and cooked through. If necessary, cover with foil to prevent it from browning too much.

Serve with cucumber and mint salad.

BUTTER MISO MUSHROOM RISOTTO

A modern Japanese twist on an Italian classic. This versatile risotto can also be made with other vegetables, such as squash and snow peas.

SERVES: 4

Preparation time: 5 minutes
Cooking time: 1 hour 50 minutes (slow cooker)
35 minutes (stovetop)

1 tablespoon (15 ml) sesame oil
10½ ounces (300 g) sushi rice, rinsed
2 cloves garlic, finely chopped
2 scallions, thinly sliced, white
    and green parts kept separate
4 tablespoons (60 g) white miso paste
3½ tablespoons (¾ ounces/50 g) butter
14 oz (400 g) mixed Asian mushrooms,
    such as shiitake (stems discarded and caps
    sliced), shimeji and enoki
¾ ounces (50 g) baby spinach leaves
toasted sesame seeds, to serve

IN THE SLOW COOKER

Heat the oil in a large frying pan over medium heat. Add the rice, garlic and the white parts of the scallions and stir for 1 minute until the rice grains are well coated. Transfer to the slow cooker.

Whisk the miso paste with 3 cups (26 fl oz/ 750 ml) of boiling water until dissolved, then pour into the slow cooker. Cook on high for 1¼ hours, stirring halfway through.

Melt 1½ tablespoons (¾ oz/20 g) of the butter in the frying pan over medium–high heat. Add the mushrooms and cook for 3 minutes until slightly softened.

Tip the mushrooms into the slow cooker, along with ¾ cup (6 fl oz/185 ml) of boiling water. Stir well, then cook for 15 minutes. Stir in the remaining butter and the spinach leaves, plus another ¾ cup (6 fl oz/185 ml) of boiling water if needed, and cook for 10 to 15 minutes until the spinach wilts and the rice is al dente. Check the seasoning.

Scatter with the green parts of the scallions and toasted sesame seeds to serve.

ON THE STOVETOP

Melt 1½ tablespoons (¾ oz/20 g) of the butter in a large, deep frying pan over medium–high heat and cook the mushrooms for 3 minutes until slightly softened. Remove and set aside.

Reduce the heat to medium and add the oil to the pan. Add the rice, garlic and the white parts of the scallions and stir for 1 minute until the rice grains are well coated.

Whisk the miso paste with 3 cups (26 fl oz/ 750 ml) of boiling water until dissolved. Add a ladleful of this miso stock to the pan and cook until the liquid has been absorbed before adding another ladleful. Continue adding the miso stock until the rice is almost al dente. Stir in the remaining butter, spinach leaves and mushrooms, plus another ¾ cup (6 fl oz/185 ml) of boiling water if needed, and cook for 5 minutes until the spinach wilts and the rice is al dente. Check the seasoning.

Scatter with the green parts of the scallions and toasted sesame seeds to serve.

LENTIL AND MUSHROOM MOUSSAKA

SERVES: 6

Preparation time: 20 minutes
Cooking time: 4¾ hours (slow cooker)
1¾ hours (oven)

¾ cup (5¾ oz/160 g) puy-style lentils
2 lb 12 oz (1.2 kg) eggplants,
    cut into ¼ inch (5 mm) slices
2 tablespoons (30 ml) olive oil, plus extra for
    brushing
1 onion, finely chopped
2 cloves garlic, finely chopped
14 ounces (400 g) portobello mushrooms,
    cut into ½ inch (1 cm) dice
2 tablespoons (8 g) finely chopped oregano
2 tablespoons (8 g) finely chopped parsley
½ teaspoon ground cinnamon
1 lb 9 oz (700 g) tomato passata
3½ tablespoons (1¾ oz/50 g) butter
⅓ cup (1¾ oz/50 g) all-purpose flour
2 cups (17 fl oz/500 ml) milk
1 egg, lightly beaten
3½ ounces (100 g) feta, crumbled
parsley and arugula leaves, to serve

IN THE SLOW COOKER

Add the lentils to a pan of water. Bring to a boil and cook for 10 minutes, then drain.

Meanwhile, preheat the broiler to high and line a large baking sheet with foil. Lightly brush the eggplant with oil, season well and grill for 5 minutes each side until golden. Set aside.

Heat the oil in a frying pan over medium–high heat. Cook the onion, garlic, mushrooms, oregano, parsley and cinnamon for about 8 minutes until the onion is soft. Stir in the passata and lentils, then season and set aside.

Melt the butter in a saucepan over medium heat. Whisk in the flour and cook for a minute, then gradually whisk in the milk. Cook for 4 minutes, stirring constantly, until the sauce thickens. Season to taste, then remove from the heat and whisk in the egg.

Lightly grease the slow cooker. Cover the base with a third of the eggplant slices, then spread over half the lentil mixture. Repeat the layers, finishing with eggplant. Pour over the sauce and scatter with the cheese, then cook on low for 4 hours. Serve with parsley and arugula leaves.

IN THE OVEN

Preheat the oven to 350°F/gas mark 4 (180°C) and grease a large baking dish. Add the lentils to a pan of water. Bring to a boil and cook for 10 minutes, then drain.

Meanwhile, preheat the broiler to high and line a large baking sheet with foil. Lightly brush the eggplant with oil, season well and grill for 5 minutes each side until golden. Set aside.

Heat the oil in a frying pan over medium–high heat. Cook the onion, garlic, mushrooms, oregano, parsley and cinnamon for about 8 minutes until the onion is soft. Stir in the passata and lentils, then season and set aside.

Melt the butter in a saucepan over medium heat. Whisk in the flour and cook for a minute, then gradually whisk in the milk. Cook for 4 minutes, stirring constantly, until the sauce thickens. Season to taste, then remove from the heat and whisk in the egg.

Cover the base of the baking dish with a third of the eggplant slices, then spread over half the lentil mixture. Repeat the layers, finishing with eggplant. Pour over the sauce and scatter with the cheese, then cover with foil and bake for 30 minutes. Carefully remove the foil, then return to the oven for another 30 minutes. Serve with parsley and arugula leaves.

SWEET AND SOUR SOYBEANS

You can find dried soybeans at Asian supermarkets and health food shops. This easy recipe is a handy one to have up your sleeve as a vegan and gluten-free option.

SERVES: 4

Preparation time: 5 minutes + overnight soaking
Cooking time: 5 hours (slow cooker)
1¼ hours (stovetop)

2 cups (15½ oz/440 g) dried soybeans,
   soaked overnight, drained and rinsed
1 carrot, cut into ½ inch (1 cm) dice
½ cup (4 fl oz/125 ml) rice wine vinegar
4 tablespoons (60 ml) rice syrup
3 tablespoons (45 ml) Chinese rice wine
2 tablespoons (30 ml) tamari sauce
1½ tablespoons (12 g) finely shredded ginger
2 teaspoons sesame oil
chopped cucumber, snow pea shoots, toasted
   sesame seeds and steamed rice, to serve

IN THE SLOW COOKER

Put the soybeans in the slow cooker with 3 cups (26 fl oz/750 ml) of water and cook on high for 4 hours. Stir in the carrot and cook for a further hour.

Drain the soybeans and carrot, then return to the slow cooker. Add the remaining ingredients and cook for 1 hour until the beans and carrot are tender.

Serve with cucumber, snow pea shoots, sesame seeds and steamed rice.

ON THE STOVETOP

Put the soybeans in a saucepan and cover with cold water. Bring to a boil, then reduce the heat to a simmer and cook for 45 minutes until almost tender. Add the carrot and cook for a further 15 minutes until tender.

Drain the soybeans and carrot and return to the pan. Add the remaining ingredients and cook for 5 minutes until warmed through.

Serve with cucumber, snow pea shoots, sesame seeds and steamed rice.

THREE CHEESE AND SWISS CHARD CANNELLONI

SERVES: 4–6

Preparation time: 20 minutes
Cooking time: 3¼ hours (slow cooker)
1 hour (oven)

4 tablespoons (60 ml) extra virgin olive oil
1 lb 10 oz (750 g) Swiss chard,
 leaves finely shredded, stems finely chopped
1 small red onion, finely chopped
3 cloves garlic, finely chopped
large handful basil, stems finely chopped,
 leaves coarsely chopped
2 tablespoons (30 g) tomato paste
2 cans (14 ounces each/400 g) chopped
 tomatoes
14 ounces (400 g) ricotta
1 cup (3½ oz/100 g) finely grated parmesan,
 plus extra to serve
4¼ ounces (120 g) bocconcini or mozzarella,
 cut into small cubes
1 egg, lightly beaten
9 ounces (250 g) cannelloni tubes

IN THE SLOW COOKER

Heat 1 tablespoon (15 ml) of the oil in a large frying pan over medium–high heat. Cook the chard stems and onion for 2 minutes, then add the chard leaves and cook for a further 2 minutes until wilted. Drain, squeezing out any excess liquid. Transfer to a large bowl and allow to cool.

Meanwhile, heat the remaining oil in a saucepan over medium–low heat. Add the garlic and basil stems and cook for 3 minutes until golden. Stir in the tomato paste and cook for a minute before adding the chopped tomatoes. Season with salt and pepper, then simmer for 10 minutes until thickened slightly. Transfer 1 cup (9 fl oz/ 250 ml) of the sauce to the slow cooker.

Add the cheeses, egg and basil leaves to the bowl with the chard and mix well. Season with salt and pepper, then transfer to a

disposable piping bag or zip-lock bag. Snip off the corner and fill the cannelloni tubes, then place in the slow cooker. Pour over the remaining tomato sauce and cook on low for 3 hours until the pasta is tender.

Serve with extra grated parmesan.

IN THE OVEN

Preheat the oven to 315°F/gas mark 2–3 (160°C). Heat 3 tablespoons (45 ml) of the oil in a saucepan over medium–low heat. Add the garlic and basil stems and cook for 3 minutes until golden. Stir in the tomato paste and cook for a minute before adding the chopped tomatoes. Season with salt and pepper, then simmer for 10 minutes until thickened slightly. Transfer 1 cup (9 fl oz/ 250 ml) of the sauce to a large baking dish.

Meanwhile, heat the remaining oil in a large frying pan over medium-high heat. Cook the chard stems and onion for 2 minutes, then add the chard leaves and cook for a further 2 minutes until wilted. Drain, squeezing out any excess liquid. Transfer to a large bowl and allow to cool.

Add the cheeses, egg and basil leaves to the bowl with the chard and mix well. Season with salt and pepper, then transfer to a disposable piping bag or zip-lock bag. Snip off the corner and fill the cannelloni tubes, then place in the dish. Pour over the remaining tomato sauce, then cover tightly with foil and bake for 30 minutes. Carefully remove the foil, then return to the oven for another 10 minutes until the pasta is tender.

Serve with extra grated parmesan.

slow
weekends

QUINOA AND CHIA PORRIDGE

This beautifully light, protein-packed porridge will sustain you all morning. You can mix up the fruit based on what you have: Try swapping the apples for pears, or raspberries for blueberries. Almond milk, quinoa flakes, chia seeds and rice malt syrup can be found in larger supermarkets and health food shops.

SERVES: 4

Preparation time: 10 minutes
Cooking time: 2 hours (slow cooker)
25 minutes (stovetop)

4 cups (35 fl oz/1 L) unsweetened almond milk
2 granny smith apples, peeled, coarsely grated
1 vanilla bean, split, seeds scraped
¾ cup (2¼ oz/60 g) quinoa flakes
3 tablespoons chia seeds
3 tablespoons (35 g) finely chopped dates
3 tablespoons (35 g) dried cherries, cranberries or chopped dried apricots
rice malt syrup or honey, raspberries and toasted slivered almonds, to serve

IN THE SLOW COOKER

Put all the ingredients into the slow cooker and cook on low for 2 hours.

Remove the vanilla bean, then serve the porridge with rice malt syrup or honey, raspberries and toasted slivered almonds.

ON THE STOVETOP

Put the almond milk, apples, dates, vanilla bean and seeds in a saucepan over low heat. Cook for 20 minutes until the apple starts to break down. Add the remaining ingredients and cook for 5 minutes until thickened.

Remove the vanilla bean, then serve the porridge with rice malt syrup or honey, raspberries and toasted slivered almonds.

BREAKFAST CURRY

This curry has just the right amount of spice to kick-start your day.

SERVES: 4

Preparation time: 10 minutes
Cooking time: 7 hours (slow cooker)
1 hour (stovetop)

1½ tablespoons (¾ oz/20 g) ghee or butter
2 sprigs curry leaves
2 teaspoons brown mustard seeds
3 teaspoons finely grated fresh turmeric
   or 1 teaspoon ground turmeric
1 red onion, finely grated
1 tablespoon (8 g) finely grated ginger
½ teaspoon ground fennel
1 teaspoon ground cumin
1 teaspoon ground coriander
1 lb 2 oz (500 g) waxy potatoes,
   cut into 1¼ inch (3 cm) cubes
3 vine-ripened tomatoes, halved,
   coarsely grated, skins discarded
1 cup (5 oz/140 g) frozen peas
8 eggs
sliced green chili and cilantro sprigs, to serve

IN THE SLOW COOKER

Put all the ingredients except the peas and eggs into the slow cooker. Add ½ cup (4 fl oz/125 ml) of water and mix well. Season with salt and pepper, then cook on low for 7 hours. Stir in the peas and cook for a further 5 minutes until warmed through.

Meanwhile, poach the eggs in a pan of simmering water until done to your liking.

Serve the curry topped with the poached eggs, sliced chili and cilantro sprigs.

ON THE STOVETOP

Heat the ghee in a large saucepan over medium heat. Add the curry leaves, mustard seeds, turmeric, onion, ginger, fennel, cumin and coriander and cook, stirring, for about 5 minutes until the onion has softened. Add the potatoes, tomatoes and ½ cup (4 fl oz/125 ml) of water and mix well. Season with salt and pepper, then cover with a lid and cook for 45 minutes, stirring occasionally. Stir in the peas and cook for a further 5 minutes until warmed through.

Meanwhile, poach the eggs in a pan of simmering water until done to your liking.

Serve the curry topped with the poached eggs, sliced chili and cilantro sprigs.

BREAKFAST FRITTATA

BREAKFAST FRITTATA

All your favorite breakfast ingredients in one dish! This is especially good made in the slow cooker, as the gentle heat gives the frittata a lovely fluffy texture.

SERVES: 4

Preparation time: 5 minutes
Cooking time: 2 hours 10 minutes (slow cooker)
30 minutes (oven)

2 teaspoons olive oil
2 breakfast sausages, casings removed
5½ ounces (150 g) pancetta, cut into lardons
3½ ounces (100 g) baby spinach leaves
1 potato, finely grated
8 eggs, lightly beaten
1 cup (3½ oz/100 g) coarsely grated
   cheddar cheese
diced tomato, sliced avocado and
   chopped chives, to serve

IN THE SLOW COOKER

Grease the slow cooker and line with parchment paper.

Heat the oil in a frying pan over medium–high heat. Cook the sausages and pancetta for 5 minutes until golden, breaking up the sausage with a wooden spoon. Transfer to the slow cooker.

Add the spinach to the frying pan and cook for 1 minute until wilted. Transfer to a sieve, along with the grated potato, and squeeze out excess moisture. Transfer to the slow cooker with the remaining ingredients and mix well. Season with salt and pepper, then cook on low for 2 hours until set.

Serve with diced tomato, sliced avocado and chopped chives.

IN THE OVEN

Preheat the oven to 325°F/gas mark 3 (170°C). Grease and line a 6 cup (52 fl oz/ 1.5 L) baking dish or roasting tin.

Heat the oil in a frying pan over medium–high heat. Cook the sausages and pancetta for 5 minutes until golden, breaking up the sausage with a wooden spoon. Transfer to the prepared dish or tin.

Add the spinach to the frying pan and cook for 1 minute until wilted. Transfer to a sieve, along with the grated potato, and squeeze out excess moisture. Transfer to the dish or pan with the remaining ingredients and mix well. Season with salt and pepper, then cook in the oven for 20 minutes until set.

Serve with diced tomato, sliced avocado and chopped chives.

REUBEN SANDWICHES

This legendary New York deli-style sandwich makes an impressive weekend lunch for family and friends.

SERVES: 4

Preparation time: 5 minutes
Cooking time: 8 hours (slow cooker)
2 hours (stovetop)

2 lb 12 oz (1.2 kg) corned beef brisket
4 fresh or dried bay leaves
1 teaspoon allspice berries
6 cloves garlic, bruised
1 teaspoon freshly ground black pepper
rye bread, Swiss cheese, sauerkraut
    and pickles, to serve

Russian dressing
1 cup (9 fl oz/250 ml) mayonnaise
2 teaspoons Tabasco sauce
1 teaspoon Worcestershire sauce
3 tablespoons (30 g) finely chopped red onion
2 teaspoons finely grated horseradish

IN THE SLOW COOKER

Put the brisket, bay leaves, allspice, garlic and pepper into the slow cooker, then pour in enough water to completely cover the meat. Cook on low for 8 hours until tender.

Meanwhile, for the Russian dressing, combine all of the ingredients in a bowl and set aside until needed.

Serve on rye bread with Russian dressing, Swiss cheese, sauerkraut and pickles.

ON THE STOVETOP

Put the brisket, bay leaves, allspice, garlic and pepper into a large, heavy-based saucepan, then pour in enough water to completely cover the meat. Bring to a boil, then reduce the heat to a simmer. Cover with a lid and cook for 2 hours until tender.

Meanwhile, for the Russian dressing, combine all of the ingredients in a bowl and set aside until needed.

Slice the corned beef and serve on rye bread with Russian dressing, Swiss cheese, sauerkraut and pickles.

BRAZILIAN FEIJOADA

This is an introductory version of the Brazilian national dish. The traditional garnish of toasted cassava flour adds another texture, but it's not essential.

SERVES: 6–8
Preparation time: 10 minutes + overnight soaking
Cooking time: 10½ hours (slow cooker)
2½ hours (stovetop)

1 lb 2 oz (500 g) black beans, soaked overnight
1 smoked ham hock
9 ounces (250 g) speck or smoked bacon, cut into ¾ inch (2 cm) pieces
2 chorizo sausages, coarsely chopped
1 lb 2 oz (500 g) pork neck, thickly sliced
6 fresh or dried bay leaves
1 tablespoon (15 ml) extra virgin olive oil
1 onion, finely chopped
4 cloves garlic, finely chopped
2 jalapeños or long green chilies, finely chopped
2 tablespoons (16 g) cornstarch – only needed for slow cooker
steamed white rice, toasted cassava flour, Tuscan kale or Swiss chard, orange slices and cilantro, to serve

IN THE SLOW COOKER

Put the beans and ham hock in a large saucepan and cover with 9 cups (79 fl oz/2.25 L) of water. Bring to a boil and cook for 10 minutes, skimming any scum from the surface. Transfer to the slow cooker, along with the speck, chorizo, pork, bay leaves, oil, onion, garlic and chilies. Stir well, then cook on low for 9 hours.

Remove the ham hock and 2 cups (17 fl oz/500 ml) of beans, then ladle a spoonful of the cooking liquid into a bowl. Set aside the ham hock until cool enough to handle. Roughly mash the beans with the back of a fork. Add the cornstarch to the liquid and whisk until smooth. Return the mashed beans and the cornstarch mixture to the slow cooker and stir well. Turn the slow cooker up to high before replacing the lid.

Roughly shred the meat from the ham hock, discarding the skin and bones. Stir the ham into the slow cooker, then cook for a further hour. Season to taste with salt.

Serve with rice, toasted cassava flour, kale, orange slices and cilantro.

ON THE STOVETOP

Put the beans, ham hock, speck, chorizo, pork and bay leaves into a large, heavy-based saucepan and cover with 9 cups (79 fl oz/2.25 L) of water. Bring to a boil, then reduce the heat to a simmer and cook for 1 hour, skimming off any scum.

Heat the oil in a frying pan over medium heat. Cook the onion, garlic and chilies for 5 minutes until the onion starts to soften. Using a slotted spoon, remove 2 cups (17 fl oz/500 ml) of beans from the saucepan and add to the onion mixture. Roughly mash, then tip the contents of the frying pan back into the saucepan and stir well.

Cover and cook for an hour, then remove the ham hock. When it is cool enough to handle, roughly shred the meat, discarding the skin and bones. Return the ham to the pan and stir well. Cook, uncovered, for 15 minutes to thicken, then season with salt.

Serve with rice, toasted cassava flour, kale, orange slices and cilantro.

PORK BELLY RAMEN

You need a large slow cooker here; if yours has a capacity of less than 6 quarts (210 fl oz/6 L) then cook the pork belly on the stovetop instead.

SERVES: 6

Preparation time: 10 minutes
Cooking time: 7 hours 45 minutes (slow cooker)
2 hours 50 minutes (stovetop)

1 tablespoon (15 ml) sesame oil, plus extra to taste
4 cloves garlic, finely chopped
1½ inch (4 cm) piece ginger, sliced
1 leek, white part only, halved, thinly sliced
1 carrot, coarsely chopped
4 cups (35 fl oz/1 L) chicken stock
1 lb 10 oz (750 g) pork leg bones, chopped into pieces (ask the butcher to do this), soaked in cold water for 1 hour
2 tablespoons (30 ml) tamari sauce
2 tablespoons (30 ml) sake
2 tablespoons (30 ml) mirin
2 teaspoons raw sugar
3½ ounces (100 g) white miso paste
1 piece kombu seaweed – optional
2 lb 4 oz (1 kg) piece lean pork belly, skin on
1 lb 2 oz (500g) ramen noodles
boiled eggs, scallion, nori, black sesame seeds and Japanese pickles, to garnish

IN THE SLOW COOKER

Heat the oil in a large, heavy-based saucepan over medium–high heat and cook the garlic, ginger, leek and carrot for 3 minutes until lightly golden. Transfer to the slow cooker.

Add the stock, pork bones and 10 cups (87 fl oz/2.5 L) of water to the pan. Bring to a boil, then simmer for 30 minutes, skimming off any froth. You should have 8 cups (70 fl oz/2 L) of stock after simmering – add more water, if needed, before transferring to the slow cooker.

Stir in the tamari, sake, mirin, sugar and miso, then add the kombu and pork belly, ensuring the meat is fully submerged.

Cook on low for 7 hours until the pork is tender. Remove and set aside until cool enough to handle. Strain the stock through a fine sieve.

Cook the noodles according to the package instructions. Remove the skin from the pork belly, then cut the meat into ½ inch (1 cm) slices.

Serve the noodles, pork belly and stock in bowls, garnished with boiled eggs, scallions, nori, sesame seeds and pickles.

ON THE STOVETOP

Heat the oil in a large, heavy-based saucepan over medium–high heat and cook the garlic, ginger, leek and carrot for 3 minutes until lightly golden. Remove and set aside.

Add the stock, pork bones and 10 cups (87 fl oz/2.5 L) of water to the pan. Bring to a boil, then simmer for 30 minutes, skimming off any scum. Return the garlic, ginger, leek and carrot to the pan and add the pork belly. Bring back to a boil, then reduce the heat to a simmer and add the tamari, sake, mirin, sugar, miso and kombu. Cook for 2 hours until the pork is tender. Remove from the pan and set aside until cool enough to handle. Strain the stock through a fine sieve.

Cook the noodles according to the package instructions. Remove the skin from the pork belly, then cut the meat into ½ inch (1 cm) slices.

Serve the noodles, pork belly and stock in bowls, garnished with boiled eggs, scallions, nori, sesame seeds and pickles.

DUCK AND MUSHROOM RAGU

SERVES: 4–6

Preparation time: 25 minutes
Cooking time: 8 hours (slow cooker)
2½ hours (stovetop)

about 2 tablespoons (30 ml) extra virgin olive oil
3 duck legs, skin removed
10½ ounces (300 g) Swiss brown or chestnut
    mushrooms, thickly sliced
1 onion, finely chopped
1 stalk celery, cut into ¼ inch (5 mm) dice
1 carrot, cut into ¼ inch (5 mm) dice
1 clove garlic, finely chopped
4 tablespoons (60 g) tomato paste
1 cup (9 fl oz/250 ml) light red wine,
    such as pinot noir
1 can (14 ounces/400 g) chopped tomatoes
3 sprigs rosemary, tied together with string
2 fresh or dried bay leaves
¾ ounces (20 g) dried porcini mushrooms, soaked
    in 1½ cups (13 fl oz/375 ml) hot water until soft
trofie or other pasta, finely grated parmesan and
    basil leaves, to serve

IN THE SLOW COOKER

Heat 1 tablespoon (15 ml) of the oil in a large,
heavy-based frying pan over medium–high
heat. Season the duck legs well with salt and
pepper, then sear for 2 minutes each side
until browned. Transfer to the slow cooker.

Add the remaining oil to the frying pan. Cook
the mushrooms, onion, celery, carrot and
garlic for 5 minutes until slightly softened,
then add the tomato paste and cook for a
further minute. Pour in the wine and cook
for 5 minutes until almost evaporated.
Transfer to the slow cooker, along with
the tomatoes, rosemary, bay leaves and the
drained porcini, plus ¾ cup (6 fl oz/185 ml)
of their soaking liquid. Cook on low for
7½ hours until the duck is very tender.

Bring a large saucepan of salted water to a
boil and cook the pasta, then drain well.

Remove the duck legs from the slow cooker.
Once they are cool enough to handle, shred
the meat, discarding the bones. Return the
duck meat to the slow cooker for 5 minutes
until warmed through. Check the seasoning.

Serve the ragu with the pasta, parmesan
and basil.

ON THE STOVETOP

Heat 1 tablespoon (15 ml) of the oil in a large,
heavy-based saucepan over medium–high
heat. Season the duck legs well with salt and
pepper, then sear for 2 minutes each side
until browned. Remove and set aside.

Add the remaining oil to the pan and cook
the mushrooms, onion, celery, carrot and
garlic for 5 minutes until slightly softened,
then add the tomato paste and cook for a
further minute. Pour in the wine and cook
for 5 minutes until almost evaporated, then
add the tomatoes, rosemary, bay leaves and
porcini with their soaking liquid. Bring to a
boil, then return the duck legs to the pan
and reduce the heat to low. Cover with a lid
and cook for 2 hours until the duck is very
tender, turning halfway through and adding
more water as needed.

Bring a large saucepan of salted water to a
boil and cook the pasta, then drain well.

Remove the duck legs from the pan. Once
they are cool enough to handle, shred the
meat, discarding the bones. Return the
duck meat to the pan and cook for 5 minutes
until warmed through. Check the seasoning.

Serve the ragu with the pasta, parmesan
and basil.

PORK AND SHRIMP POZOLE

This celebratory Mexican stew is traditionally made with dried white corn that has been soaked overnight with lime paste to make hominy. If you're lucky enough to find pre-treated, ready-to-cook hominy at a specialty food shop or Mexican deli, boil ½ cup (7 oz/200 g) for 2½ to 3 hours until the kernels are tender, and then proceed with the recipe. Otherwise, use canned hominy, or even white beans. If you have trouble getting your hands on chipotle chilies in adobo (they are usually sold in small cans), their smoky flavor can be approximated by using a mix of smoked paprika and chili flakes.

SERVES: 4

Preparation time: 10 minutes
Cooking time: 8 hours (slow cooker)
1¾ hours (stovetop)

1 tablespoon (15 ml) olive oil – only needed
   for stovetop
1 can (1 lb 12 oz/800 g) hominy, drained
750 g (1 lb 10 oz) pork neck,
   cut into 1 inch (2.5 cm) cubes
4 cloves garlic, minced
1 white or brown onion, finely grated
4 tomatoes, halved, coarsely grated,
   skins discarded
2 cups (17 fl oz/500 ml) chicken stock
2 chipotle chilies in adobo, finely chopped
1 jalapeño chili, seeds removed, finely chopped
1 tablespoon (3 g) dried oregano
12 large raw shrimp, peeled and deveined, tails
   left intact
finely grated zest and juice of 1 lime
finely sliced radishes, shredded cabbage,
   cilantro sprigs, lime halves and corn chips,
   to serve

IN THE SLOW COOKER

Put the hominy into the slow cooker with the pork, garlic, onion, tomatoes, stock, chilies and oregano. Season to taste with salt and pepper, then cook on low for 8 hours until the corn and pork are tender.

Add the shrimp, lime zest and juice and cook for a further 5 minutes until the shrimp are just cooked.

Serve the pozole with finely sliced radishes, shredded cabbage, cilantro sprigs, lime halves and corn chips.

ON THE STOVETOP

Heat the oil in a large frying pan over medium–high heat. Season the pork with salt, then sear for 5 minutes until browned. Remove and set aside. Add the garlic and onion to the pan and cook for 5 minutes until softened. Turn off the heat.

Put the hominy into a large saucepan with the pork, garlic, onion, tomatoes, stock, chilies and oregano. Bring to a boil, then reduce the heat to a simmer and cook for 1½ hours until the pork and corn are tender.

Add the shrimp, lime zest and juice and cook for a further 5 minutes until the shrimp are just cooked. Season to taste with salt and pepper.

Serve the pozole with finely sliced radishes, shredded cabbage, cilantro sprigs, lime halves and corn chips.

PERSIAN LAMB SHANKS WITH BROAD BEAN AND DILL RICE

You'll need a large slow cooker to accommodate the lamb shanks, but this tender lamb dish is every bit as good cooked in the oven. Find dried limes and dried fenugreek leaves (also called methi) at specialty food shops or online.

SERVES: 6

Preparation time: 20 minutes + overnight soaking
Cooking time: 10¼ hours (slow cooker)
2¾ hours (oven)

1 tablespoon (15 ml) olive oil
6 small lamb shanks
1 cup (6½ oz/185 g) dried black-eyed peas,
   soaked overnight, drained and rinsed
3 cloves garlic, crushed
6 dried limes, pricked with a fork
3 tablespoons (9 g) dried fenugreek leaves
2 teaspoons ground turmeric
1 tablespoon (3 g) dried mint
6 scallions, thinly sliced,
   paler and green parts kept separate
4 cups (10½ oz/300 g) shredded kale leaves

Broad bean and dill rice
4 tablespoons (60 ml) extra virgin olive oil
4 tablespoons (2 oz/60 g) butter
3 cloves garlic, crushed
2 cups (14 oz/400 g) basmati rice, cooked
1 lb 2 oz (500 g) frozen broad beans, thawed
2 large handfuls coarsely chopped dill

IN THE SLOW COOKER

Heat the oil in a large frying pan over medium–high heat. Season the lamb shanks with salt and sear for 5 minutes to brown.

In the slow cooker, combine the black-eyed peas, garlic, dried limes, fenugreek, turmeric, mint, the paler parts of the scallions and 3 cups (26 fl oz/750 ml) of water. Add the lamb shanks, season with salt and pepper, and cook on low for 9 hours. Stir in the scallion greens and kale and cook for 1 hour.

For the broad bean and dill rice, heat the oil and butter in a saucepan over medium heat, then cook the garlic for 2 to 3 minutes until golden. Stir in the rice, broad beans and dill and cook for 2 minutes to warm through.

Serve the lamb shanks with the rice.

IN THE OVEN

Preheat the oven to 315°F/gas mark 2–3 (160°C). Heat the oil in a large, flameproof casserole over medium–high heat. Season the lamb shanks with salt and sear for 5 minutes to brown, then set aside. Add the black-eyed peas, garlic, dried limes, fenugreek, turmeric, mint, the paler parts of the scallions and 4 cups (35 fl oz/1 L) of water. Season with salt and pepper and bring to a boil, then return the lamb shanks to the casserole. Cut out a circle of parchment paper to fit the casserole and lay it directly on the lamb. Cook in the oven for 2 hours, turning the shanks halfway through. Stir in the scallion greens and kale and return to the oven for 30 minutes until the lamb is tender.

For the broad bean and dill rice, heat the oil and butter in a saucepan over medium heat, then cook the garlic for 2 to 3 minutes until golden. Stir in the rice, broad beans and dill and cook for 2 minutes to warm through.

Serve the lamb shanks with the rice.

LAMB BIRYANI

SERVES: 4

Preparation time: 10 minutes
Cooking time: 6¼ hours (slow cooker)
1½ hours (stovetop)

2 tablespoons (30 ml) grapeseed or rice bran oil
1 lb 10 oz (750 g) lamb neck,
    cut into ¾ inch (2 cm) pieces
2½ tablespoons (1½ oz/40 g) ghee or butter
2 small red onions, halved, thinly sliced
3 tablespoons (25 g) finely grated ginger
6 cloves garlic, finely chopped
2 cinnamon sticks
1½ teaspoons ground turmeric
2 teaspoons garam masala
1 teaspoon ground chili
2 teaspoons green cardamom pods, cracked
2 tomatoes, halved, coarsely grated,
    skins discarded
1¾ ounces (50 g) raisins
½ cup (4¾ oz/130 g) Greek-style yogurt
2 cups (14 oz/400 g) basmati rice
½ teaspoon saffron threads, soaked in
    2 teaspoons hot water
roasted cashews, mint leaves and cilantro sprigs,
    to serve

IN THE SLOW COOKER

Heat the oil in a large, heavy-based frying pan over medium–high heat. Season the lamb with salt, then sear for 5 minutes to brown. Transfer to the slow cooker.

Add the ghee to the frying pan and cook the onions, ginger, garlic, cinnamon, turmeric, garam masala, chili and 1 teaspoon of the cardamom pods for 5 minutes until fragrant, stirring so the spices don't burn. Transfer to the slow cooker, along with the tomatoes, raisins and yogurt. Cook on low for 6 hours until the lamb is tender.

When the lamb is almost ready, cook the rice in salted boiling water with the remaining cardamom pods until tender.

Drain. Put half the rice into a bowl and stir through the saffron and its soaking liquid. Keep warm.

Spoon half the plain rice onto a platter, then half the saffron rice. Spoon the lamb over the top, followed by the remaining plain rice and then the remaining saffron rice.

Serve with roasted cashews, mint leaves and cilantro sprigs.

ON THE STOVETOP

Heat the oil in a large, heavy-based saucepan over medium–high heat. Season the lamb with salt and sear for 5 minutes to brown. Remove and set aside. Add the ghee to the pan, together with the onions, ginger, garlic, cinnamon, turmeric, garam masala, chili and 1 teaspoon of the cardamom pods. Cook for 5 minutes until fragrant, stirring so the spices don't burn. Stir in the tomatoes, raisins and yogurt, then return the lamb to the pan and reduce the heat to low. Cook for 1¼ hours until the lamb is tender, stirring occasionally.

When the lamb is almost ready, cook the rice in salted boiling water with the remaining cardamom pods until tender. Drain. Put half the rice into a bowl and stir through the saffron and its soaking liquid. Keep warm.

Spoon half the plain rice onto a platter, then half the saffron rice. Spoon the lamb over the top, followed by the remaining plain rice and then the remaining saffron rice.

Serve with roasted cashews, mint leaves and cilantro sprigs.

sweet
things

ORANGE AND POPPY SEED CAKE

This gluten-free cake was made in a 6-quart (192 fl oz/5.5 L) slow cooker. If your slow cooker is larger or smaller than this, the cooking time may vary, so keep an eye on your cake for the last hour or so.

SERVES: 8
Preparation time: 10 minutes
Cooking time: 3¾ hours (slow cooker)
1¼ hours (oven)

2 cups (7 oz/200g) ground almonds
1 cup (4¼ oz/120 g) quinoa flour
2½ teaspoons baking powder
4 tablespoons (25 g) poppy seeds
finely grated zest and juice of 2 oranges –
   you need 1 cup (9 fl oz/250 ml) juice
½ cup (4 fl oz/125 ml) light olive oil
½ cup (4¾ oz/130 g) Greek-style yogurt
¾ cup (6 fl oz/185 ml) honey
1 teaspoon vanilla extract
3 eggs, lightly beaten

Candied oranges and syrup
juice of 1 large orange
4 tablespoons (85 g) honey
1 large orange, thinly sliced

IN THE SLOW COOKER

Grease the slow cooker and line with parchment paper. Cover the lid of the slow cooker with a clean tea towel, securing the corners around the knob with string or an elastic band. This is to prevent condensation dripping onto the cake as it cooks.

Combine the almonds, flour, baking powder and poppy seeds in a large bowl. In another bowl, whisk together the orange zest and juice, oil, yogurt, honey, vanilla and eggs, then gradually whisk into the almond mixture to make a batter.

Pour the cake batter into the slow cooker and cook on low for 3 hours until a skewer inserted into the center comes out clean.

Turn off the slow cooker but leave the cake in it for another 30 minutes.

For the candied oranges and syrup, put the orange juice and and honey in a small, non-reactive pan. Bring to a boil, then reduce the heat to medium. Add the orange slices and cook for 5 minutes each side until the oranges shrink and caramelize.

Carefully remove the cake and top with the candied oranges and syrup.

IN THE OVEN

Preheat the oven to 350°F/gas mark 4 (180°C) and grease and line a 9½ inch (24 cm) cake pan.

Combine the almonds, flour, baking powder and poppy seeds in a large bowl.
In another bowl, whisk together the orange zest and juice, oil, yogurt, honey, vanilla and eggs, then gradually whisk into the almond mixture to make a batter.

Pour the cake batter into the pan and bake for 55 minutes until a skewer inserted into the center comes out clean. Cover the cake with foil if it browns too quickly.

For the candied oranges and syrup, put the orange juice and and honey in a small, non-reactive pan. Bring to a boil, then reduce the heat to medium. Add the orange slices and cook for 5 minutes each side until the oranges shrink and caramelize.

Carefully turn out the cake and top with the candied oranges and syrup.

APPLE AND
BLUEBERRY CAKE

APPLE AND BLUEBERRY CAKE

To make this dessert completely dairy-free, drizzle with coconut cream instead of serving with mascarpone.

SERVES: 8

Preparation time: 15 minutes
Cooking time: 3 hours (slow cooker)
1¼ hours (oven)

2 lb 4 oz (1 kg) granny smith apples, quartered, cores removed, cut into very thin slices
1 teaspoon mixed spice
3 eggs
1 cup (5½ oz/155 g) coconut sugar
1 cup (9 fl oz/250 ml) melted coconut oil
3 tablespoons (45 ml) agave syrup or mild honey
1 vanilla bean, split, seeds scraped
1 cup (5½ oz/150 g) all-purpose flour, sifted
4½ ounces (125 g) fresh or frozen blueberries
mascarpone, to serve

IN THE SLOW COOKER

Lightly oil the slow cooker. In a bowl, combine the apples with the mixed spice, then evenly layer them in the slow cooker.

Using an electric mixer, beat the eggs and sugar until pale and thick, then beat in the coconut oil, syrup and vanilla seeds until combined. Using a spatula or large metal spoon, gently fold in the flour, followed by the blueberries.

Pour the batter onto the apples to cover. Cook on high for 2½ hours, then turn off the slow cooker and set aside for 30 minutes before removing.

Serve with mascarpone.

IN THE OVEN

Preheat the oven to 350°F/gas mark 4 (180°C). Lightly oil and line a 6–8 cup (52–70 fl oz/1.5–2 L) pie dish. In a bowl, combine the apples with the mixed spice, then evenly layer them in the dish.

Using an electric mixer, beat the eggs and sugar until pale and thick, then beat in the coconut oil, syrup and vanilla seeds until combined. Using a spatula or large metal spoon, gently fold in the flour, followed by the blueberries.

Pour the batter onto the apples to cover, then bake for 1 hour until a skewer inserted in the center comes out clean. Remove and set aside to cool for about 10 minutes.

Serve with mascarpone.

SELF-SAUCING DARK CHOCOLATE, FIG AND HAZELNUT PUDDING

This pudding can either be baked in the oven or made in a smaller slow cooker — a 4-quart (140 fl oz/4 L) one. Either way, with its autumnal ingredients of figs and hazelnuts, and a rich chocolate sauce, it will soon become a favorite.

SERVES: 6–8

Preparation time: 10 minutes
Cooking time: 2 hours (slow cooker)
45 minutes (oven)

½ cup (4 fl oz/125 ml) melted butter
1½ cups (8½ oz/235 g) coconut sugar
1½ cups (8 oz/225 g) self-rising flour, sifted
1 egg, lightly beaten
1 cup (9 fl oz/250 ml) almond milk
2 teaspoons vanilla extract
½ cup (2 oz/55 g) cacao powder
6 dried figs, coarsely chopped
3½ ounces (100 g) dark chocolate,
    coarsely chopped
4 tablespoons (25 g) blanched hazelnuts,
    toasted, coarsely chopped

IN THE SLOW COOKER

Lightly grease the slow cooker.

In a bowl, combine the melted butter, 1 cup (5½ oz/155 g) of the coconut sugar, flour, egg, milk, vanilla and 3 tablespoons (20 g) of the cacao. Fold in the figs, chocolate and 3 tablespoons (21 g) of the hazelnuts, then spoon into the slow cooker, spreading it out evenly. Scatter with the remaining sugar, cacao and hazelnuts. Gently pour over 2½ cups (21½ fl oz/625 ml) of boiling water and cook on low for 2 hours or until set, then serve.

IN THE OVEN

Preheat the oven to 350°F/gas mark 4 (180°C). Grease a 13 x 9-inch (33 x 23 cm) baking dish.

In a bowl, combine the melted butter, 1 cup (5½ oz/155 g) of the coconut sugar, flour, egg, milk, vanilla and 3 tablespoons (20 g) of the cacao. Fold in the figs, chocolate and 3 tablespoons (21 g) of the hazelnuts, then spoon into the dish, spreading it out evenly. Scatter with the remaining sugar, cacao and hazelnuts, then gently pour over 2½ cups (21½ fl oz/625 ml) of boiling water.

Cook in the oven for 40 minutes until set, then set aside for 5 minutes before serving.

STICKY DATE PUDDING

Who can resist a classic sticky date pudding? You need a small slow cooker for this, so if yours has a capacity greater than 4 quarts (140 fl oz/4 L), bake it instead.

SERVES: 8

Preparation time: 10 minutes +
20 minutes soaking
Cooking time: 3 hours (slow cooker)
1 hour (oven)

1½ cups (8½ oz/240 g) pitted dates,
    coarsely chopped
1 teaspoon baking soda
6 tablespoons (2¾ oz/80 g) butter
½ cup (2¾ oz/80 g) coconut sugar
4 tablespoons (60 ml) maple syrup
4 tablespoons (60 ml) light olive oil
2 eggs
1½ cups (8 oz/225 g) self-rising flour
vanilla ice cream, to serve

Caramel sauce
½ cup (4 fl oz/125 ml) maple syrup
½ cup (2¾ oz/80 g) coconut sugar
7 tablespoons (3½ oz/100 g) butter
¼ teaspoon salt

IN THE SLOW COOKER

Grease and line the slow cooker.

Put the dates and baking soda into a heatproof bowl. Pour over 1½ cups (13 fl oz/375 ml) of boiling water and set aside for 20 minutes.

Using an electric mixer, beat the butter, sugar and syrup until thick and pale. Beat in the oil, then add the eggs one at time, beating well after each addition. Gently fold in the date mixture, followed by the flour, until just combined. Spoon into the slow cooker and cook on low for 3 hours.

For the caramel sauce, put the syrup and sugar in a small saucepan over medium heat, stirring until dissolved. Add the butter and salt, stirring to melt. Once the butter has melted, reduce the heat to low and cook for 5 minutes until thickened slightly.

Carefully remove the pudding and serve with caramel sauce and ice cream.

IN THE OVEN

Preheat the oven to 350°F/gas mark 4 (180°C). Grease and line a 8½ inch (22 cm) cake pan.

Put the dates and baking of soda into a heatproof bowl. Pour over 1½ cups (13 fl oz/375 ml) of boiling water and set aside for 20 minutes.

Using an electric mixer, beat the butter, sugar and syrup until thick and pale. Beat in the oil, then add the eggs one at time, beating well after each addition. Gently fold in the date mixture, followed by the flour, until just combined.

Spoon into the prepared pan and bake for 40 minutes until a skewer inserted in the center comes out clean. Remove from the oven and set aside for 10 minutes before turning out onto a serving plate.

For the caramel sauce, put the syrup and sugar in a small saucepan over medium heat, stirring until dissolved. Add the butter and salt, stirring to melt. Once the butter has melted, reduce the heat to low and cook for 5 minutes until thickened slightly.

Serve with caramel sauce and ice cream.

TRIPLE CHOCOLATE BROWNIES

We used a large, wide-based 6-quart (210 fl oz/6 L) slow cooker to make these. If yours is a different size or shape, the cooking time may vary. Either test the brownies with a skewer a few times during the last half hour, or bake instead.

MAKES: 12

Preparation time: 15 minutes
(+ 20 minutes standing if making in slow cooker)
Cooking time: 2½ hours (slow cooker)
35 minutes (oven)

1 cup (8 oz/225 g) coconut oil
7 ounces (200 g) dark 70% chocolate, chopped
3 tablespoons (30 g) cacao powder,
     plus extra for dusting
½ cup (4 fl oz/125 ml) maple syrup
4 tablespoons (60 ml) agave syrup or mild honey
1 teaspoon vanilla extract
3 eggs, lightly beaten
¼ teaspoon salt
1 cup (5½ oz/150 g) whole-wheat
     all-purpose flour
1 teaspoon baking powder
3 tablespoons (21 g) coarsely chopped walnuts
2¾ ounces (75 g) good-quality milk chocolate,
     cut into ½ inch (1 cm) pieces

IN THE SLOW COOKER

Grease the slow cooker and line with parchment paper.

Melt the coconut oil and dark chocolate in a heatproof bowl set over a saucepan of barely simmering water. Once melted, stir in the cacao powder, maple syrup, agave syrup, vanilla extract, eggs and salt. Fold in the flour and baking powder until just combined, then stir in the walnuts and milk chocolate.

Pour into the slow cooker and cook on low for 2½ hours until cooked through when you poke a skewer into the center. Turn off the slow cooker, leaving the brownie inside for 20 minutes.

Use the parchment paper to gently lift out the brownie and cut into squares.

IN THE OVEN

Preheat the oven to 315°F/gas mark 2–3 (160°C) and line a 8½ inch (22 cm) square cake pan.

Melt the coconut oil and dark chocolate in a heatproof bowl set over a saucepan of barely simmering water. Once melted, stir in the cacao powder, maple syrup, agave syrup, vanilla extract, eggs and salt. Fold in the flour and baking powder until just combined, then stir in the walnuts and milk chocolate.

Pour the batter into the pan and bake for 35 minutes until a skewer inserted in the center comes out with a few moist crumbs attached. Set aside to cool, then remove from the pan and cut into squares.

COCONUT BROWN RICE PUDDING WITH BANANA AND GINGER

This vegan rice pudding is a real treat, with all the flavors and aromas of a vacation in the tropics: coconut, banana, ginger and kaffir lime leaves.

SERVES: 4

Preparation time: 5 minutes
Cooking time: 5 hours (slow cooker)
1 hour 40 minutes (stovetop)

1 cup (7¾ oz/220 g) medium-grain brown rice
1 can (14 fl oz/400 ml) coconut milk
3 cups (26 fl oz/750 ml) rice or almond milk
4 tablespoons (50 g) coarsely grated dark palm sugar
1 tablespoon (8 g) finely grated ginger
2 bananas, chopped
4 kaffir lime leaves
¼ teaspoon salt
sliced banana, black sesame seeds, very finely shredded kaffir lime leaves, shredded coconut and sliced brandied ginger, to serve

IN THE SLOW COOKER

Put all the ingredients into the slow cooker and cook on low for 5 hours until the rice is tender.

Serve with banana, black sesame seeds, kaffir lime leaves, coconut and ginger.

ON THE STOVETOP

Put all the ingredients into a saucepan with 2 cups (17 fl oz/500 ml) of water. Bring to a simmer over medium heat, then reduce the heat to low and cook for 1½ hours until the rice is tender, stirring regularly. Toward the end of the cooking, stir more frequently and add more water if necessary.

Serve with banana, black sesame seeds, kaffir lime leaves, coconut and ginger.

CHAI-SPICED POACHED PEARS

These tender chai-infused pears are the perfect way to end an Indian-inspired meal, such as the Southern Indian chicken curry on page 130, or perhaps a vegetarian feast of beet curry and yellow dal with spinach (see pages 134 and 123).

SERVES: 4

Preparation time: 5 minutes + 15 minutes steeping
Cooking time: 3½ hours (slow cooker)
30 minutes (stovetop)

1 cup (5½ oz/155 g) coconut sugar
3 tablespoons (60 g) honey
6 cardamom pods, cracked
2 cinnamon sticks, broken in half
8 cloves
1 teaspoon black peppercorns
1½ inch (4 cm) piece ginger, thinly sliced
4 black tea bags
4 firm pears, such as beurre bosc, halved, cores removed
vanilla ice cream and toasted pistachios, to serve

IN THE SLOW COOKER

Put the sugar, honey and spices into the slow cooker. Pour in 6 cups (52 fl oz/1.5 L) of boiling water and stir well to dissolve the sugar. Add the tea bags and set aside for 15 minutes to steep.

Remove the tea bags and discard. Add the pears to the slow cooker. Cut out a circle of parchment paper to fit the slow cooker and lay it directly on the surface of the liquid. Cook on low for about 3½ hours until the pears are tender. The exact cooking time will depend on their ripeness.

Serve the pears with vanilla ice cream and toasted pistachios.

ON THE STOVETOP

Put the sugar, honey and spices into a large saucepan. Pour in 6 cups (52 fl oz/1.5 L) of water and bring to a boil, stirring well to dissolve the sugar. Turn off the heat, add the tea bags and set aside for 15 minutes to steep.

Remove the tea bags and discard. Add the pears to the pan. Cut out a circle of parchment paper to fit the pan and lay it directly on the surface of the liquid. Bring to a simmer over low heat and cook for about 25 minutes until the pears are tender. The exact cooking time will depend on their ripeness.

Serve the pears with vanilla ice cream and toasted pistachios.

HONEY RHUBARB NUT CRUMBLE

This is gluten- and dairy-free dessert for everyone to enjoy.

SERVES: 6

Preparation time: 5 minutes
Cooking time: 2 hours (slow cooker)
1 hour (oven)

½ cup (4 fl oz/125 ml) melted coconut oil
2 bunches (1 lb 2 oz/500 g) rhubarb, trimmed,
   cut into 2 inch (5 cm) pieces
½ cup (6 oz/175 g) honey
2 teaspoons vanilla extract
1 teaspoon ground ginger
1 teaspoon ground cinnamon
1 cup (3½ oz/100 g) ground almonds
1 cup (5¾ oz/155 g) macadamia nuts (toasted
   if using slow cooker), coarsely chopped
1 cup (5¾ oz/155 g) blanched almonds
⅔ cup (2¾ oz/80 g) walnuts, toasted,
   coarsely chopped

IN THE SLOW COOKER

Lighty oil the slow cooker. Combine the rhubarb, 4 tablespoons (80 g) of the honey, vanilla, ginger and cinnamon in the slow cooker.

In a bowl, combine the remaining ingredients (including the rest of the honey) and scatter over the rhubarb mixture.

Cook the crumble on high for 2 hours.

IN THE OVEN

Preheat the oven to 350°F/gas mark 4 (180°C) and oil a 6 cups (52 fl oz/1.5 L) baking dish. Combine the rhubarb, 4 tablespoons (80 g) of the honey, vanilla, ginger and cinnamon in the prepared dish.

Cover with foil and bake for 30 minutes until the rhubarb is tender.

In a bowl, combine the remaining ingredients (including the rest of the honey) and scatter over the rhubarb mixture. Return to the oven and cook, uncovered, for 30 minutes until the crumble is golden.

PUMPKIN AND CINNAMON CHEESECAKE

This cheesecake keeps well for a few days in the fridge, and the base becomes extra gooey and delicious as it sits. Perfect with a mid-morning or after-dinner espresso.

SERVES: 8–10

Preparation time: 25 minutes
(+ 30 minutes resting if making in slow cooker)
Cooking time: 6¾ hours (slow cooker)
50 minutes (oven)

14 ounces (400 g) peeled sugar pumpkin,
   cut into 1½ inch (4 cm) cubes
1 cup (5½ oz/150 g) all-purpose flour
½ teaspoon baking powder
1 cup (5½ oz/155 g) coconut sugar
1½ sticks (5½ oz/150 g) unsalted butter, melted
4 eggs, 1 lightly beaten
9 ounces (250 g) cream cheese, softened
½ cup (4 fl oz/125 ml) maple syrup
2 teaspoons vanilla extract
2 teaspoons ground cinnamon

IN THE SLOW COOKER

Cook the pumpkin in a saucepan of boiling water for 10 minutes until tender. Drain in a colander and leave to air-dry.

Meanwhile, sift the flour and baking powder into a bowl. Add half the sugar, 3 tablespoons (1¾ oz/50 g) of the melted butter and the beaten egg and mix until a dough forms.

Grease the slow cooker and line with parchment paper. Press the dough evenly over the base of the slow cooker.

Purée the pumpkin in a food processor. Add the cream cheese, maple syrup, vanilla and cinnamon, plus the remaining sugar, and process until smooth. Add the remaining eggs, one at time, pulsing until combined. Add the remaining butter and pulse again.

Pour the cheesecake mixture into the slow cooker and cook on low for 6 hours until just set; the center should still wobble slightly. Turn off the slow cooker and leave the cheesecake to rest for 30 minutes before removing. Set aside to cool completely.

IN THE OVEN

Cook the pumpkin in a saucepan of boiling water for 10 minutes until tender. Drain in a colander and leave to air-dry.

Preheat the oven to 350°F/gas mark 4 (180°C). Grease a 9½ inch (24 cm) springform cake pan and line with parchment paper.

Meanwhile, sift the flour and baking powder into a bowl. Add half the sugar, 3 tablespoons (1¾ oz/50 g) of the melted butter and the beaten egg and mix until a dough forms. Press the dough evenly into the tin.

Purée the pumpkin in a food processor. Add the cream cheese, maple syrup, vanilla and cinnamon, plus the remaining sugar, and process until smooth. Add the remaining eggs, one at time, pulsing until combined. Add the remaining butter and pulse again.

Pour the cheesecake mixture into the pan and bake in the oven for 40 minutes until just set; the center should still wobble slightly. Set aside to cool completely.

BREAD, PEANUT BUTTER AND JAM PUDDING

You can try all different types of combinations for this, including the classic bread and butter pudding made with marmalade. You could also add chocolate chips for a more decadent dessert.

SERVES: 6

Preparation time: 15 minutes + 15 minutes soaking
Cooking time: 3 hours (slow cooker)
1 hour (oven)

⅓ cup (3¼ oz/90 g) crunchy peanut butter
½ cup (5¾ oz/165 g) raspberry jam
8 thick slices sourdough bread,
　cut in half diagonally
6 eggs
2 cups (17 fl oz/500 ml) milk
½ cup (4 fl oz/125 ml) thin (pouring) cream
½ cup (2¾ oz/80 g) coconut sugar
1 teaspoon vanilla extract

IN THE SLOW COOKER

Lightly spread the butter and half the jam over both sides of the bread slices, then arrange in the slow cooker.

Whisk the eggs, milk, cream, sugar and vanilla extract in a bowl until the sugar dissolves. Pour into the slow cooker, pressing down the bread slices to submerge them. Set aside to soak for 15 minutes, then cook on high for 3 hours until set.

In a small bowl, combine the remaining jam with 1 tablespoon (15 ml) of water. Serve the pudding drizzled with this jam syrup.

IN THE OVEN

Preheat the oven to 300°F/gas mark 2 (150°C). Lightly spread the butter and half the jam over both sides of the bread slices, then arrange in an 8–10 cup (70–104 fl oz/ 2–2.5 L) baking dish.

Whisk the eggs, milk, cream, sugar and vanilla extract in a bowl until the sugar dissolves. Pour into the dish, pressing down the bread slices to submerge them. Set aside to soak for 15 minutes.

Sit the baking dish in a large roasting pan and pour enough boiling water into the pan to come up halfway up the sides of the dish. Cover the dish with foil and bake the pudding for 30 minutes. Carefully remove the foil, then return to the oven for another 30 minutes until set.

In a small bowl, combine the remaining jam with 1 tablespoon (15 ml) of water. Serve the pudding drizzled with this jam syrup.

INDEX

U

ultimate bolognese, 28

V

veal blade: veal stroganoff, 82
veal osso buco with kale
    gremolata, 16
vegan recipes
    coconut brown rice pudding
        with banana and ginger, 225
    leek, fennel and potato
        soup, 150
    Moroccan fava bean soup, 158
    sweet and sour soybeans, 182
vegetarian options *see* meat-free
    meals
Vietnamese beef noodle soup, 50

W

white bean mash, 70

Y

yellow dal with spinach, 123

Quarto is the authority on a wide range of topics.

Quarto educates, entertains and enriches the lives of our readers—enthusiasts and lovers of hands-on living.

www.QuartoKnows.com

Text, design and photography
© Murdoch Books 2015

First published in the United States of America
in 2016 by
Fair Winds Press, an imprint of
Quarto Publishing Group USA Inc.
100 Cummings Center
Suite 406-L
Beverly, Massachusetts 01915-6101
Telephone: (978) 282-9590
Fax: (978) 283-2742
QuartoKnows.com
Visit our blogs at QuartoKnows.com

20 19 18 17 16   1 2 3 4 5

ISBN: 978-1-59233-753-8

Library of Congress Cataloging-in-Publication Data available

Printed in China

Color reproduction by Splitting Image
Color Studio Pty Ltd, Clayton, Victoria
Printed by Hang Tai Printing Company Ltd, China

IMPORTANT: Those who might be at risk from the effects of salmonella poisoning (the elderly, pregnant women, young children and those suffering from immune deficiency diseases) should consult their doctor with any concerns about eating raw eggs.

OVEN GUIDE: You may find that cooking times vary, depending on the oven you are using. For fan-forced ovens, as a general rule, set the oven temperature to 35°F (20°C) lower than indicated in the recipe.

THANK YOU: The publisher thanks the following for props used in the photography of this book:
Koskela (koskela.com.au)
Le Creuset (lecreuset.com.au)
Mud Australia (mudaustralia.com)
DI Lorenzo Tiles (dilorenzo.net.au)
1803 Artisan Deer Designs (1803.com.au)
Malcolm Greenwood
(malcolmgreenwood.com.au)
Ceramics by Anna-Karina
(annakarinaelias@gmail.com)
Susan Simonini (susansimonini.com.au)

The information in this book is for educational purposes only. It is not intended to replace the advice of a physician or medical practitioner. Please see your health-care provider before beginning any new health program.